PSYCHIC EMPATH HEALING

Empath Survival Guide To Becoming A Healer
Instead Of Absorbing Negative Energies. The Life
Strategies Of Sensitive People, And Activate
Hidden Superpowers To Develop Abilities

By

DANIEL BRIAN

About The Author

Daniel Brian is an America based psychologist who holds a Ph.D. degree in clinical psychology. He has conducted many essential pieces of research in post-traumatic stress disorder, emotional regulatory disorders, substance abuse. He has practiced clinical psychology for more than 20 years and became a leading voice for many empaths and psychologist.

Being a passionate clinician, he stresses the need for psychotherapy in people suffering from stress disorders and he plays his part in excelling in this field. His line of interest was always human traits and how they affect their personality and regulate their emotions.

He also worked on neuroscience and related psychotherapy with neurologic aspects. His recent writings emphasize the evolutionary changes in the human brain which react with hormones and respond respectively.

This American psychologist stated that he was influenced by the field of psychiatry which tells exceptional stories and shows you the mental health of the individual. He combines his knowledge of emotional intelligence with neuroscience to demonstrate how to stay strong and powerful while being compassionate and empathic.

He included such stories in his book as he believed in emotional strengths that can regulate moods and feelings and also bought positive changes to many of his patients. His other works include empaths and healing soon after he realized the importance of balancing emotions and survival after trauma. As a practitioner of clinical psychology, he helps people out of the grip of their inner demons and encourages them to set healthy boundaries and know their sensitivities.

Table of Contents

INTRODUCTION

Empathy has a broad scope of meanings and definitions. Usually, most concepts share the chance of an individual's response to their opinion of another person's present perception. Its English linguistic usage is new, showcasing around the inception of the twentieth century, now and then in craftsmanship discussions. Its causes followed the German word 'Einfuhlung,' which genuinely represents "feeling into" (as in envisioning oneself into something else). Other than researching the field of social science, the analysis of sympathy has moreover figured unquestionably in client-focused psychotherapy. There is much discussion about the difference between sympathy and empathy, yet people use both terms on an overlapping basis. Empathy has a broad scope of meanings and definitions. Usually, most concepts share the chance of an individual's response to their opinion of another person's present perception. On building the capability, an individual grasps the other individual's experiences, just like he has experienced it on his own. A separation is held among self and others. Sympathy, strangely, incorporates the test of being moved by or responding under another person. Another normal separation is to use it while mentioning unequivocally to the concerned side of compassion.

Inside social mind science, it may suggest an energetic or mental understanding instinct. On the exciting side, there are three most mulled over sections of empathy. The first is feeling a comparative inclination as a target person (a portion of the time attributed to active infection, e.g., accidentally "getting" someone else's tears and getting vibes of hopelessness).

The next part, singular agony, implies one's assumptions of difficulty considering seeing another's scrape. This agony might mirror the direction that the other person is truly feeling. The third energetic section, feeling compassionate towards another person, is usually a significant part of examining compassion in cerebrum exploration. It is consistently called empathic concern and once in a while sympathy. Such concern is thought to rise later developmentally and demand more restriction than either enthusiastic ailment or individual difficulty, regardless of how these earlier sections in all likelihood lay the reason for later, progressively refined sorts of compassion.

Such concern merits one of a kind thought for its activity in initiating prosocial and assisting rehearses. Research dependably finds a valuable connection between how much empathic concern persons report feeling for target individuals and their enthusiasm to authorize those persons, to any occasion, when supporting requires some repentance.

The most reputable examples of a person's acts and words, including helping untouchables and destroyed humans, are said to have compassionate roots (regardless of how humans are the main species that helps others in a sticky situation). Shreds of studies on empathic support have incited a stimulated (and possibly never-to-be-settled) chitchat about whether such support is genuinely unselfish (impelled by an unconventional target to benefit the other individual).

Alternatively, it is convinced by comical prizes, for instance, diminishing one's difficulty realized by watching another human's condition, saving one's family (and subsequently some piece of one's characteristics), or ensuring genuine respect or the integral help later on. The way tangles attempt to pick whether the helping conduct is mindful or whimsical that moral duty and favorable circumstances to the following individual may cover.

The abstract side of empathy focuses on the outdated philosophical "various characters issue": Our thought-process and demonstration are our own alone, and we can never genuinely find a workable pace of another human's perception. Mental compassion infiltrates how much we see or prove that we have viably theorized someone else's insights.

The scope of emotional empathy joins some essential tasks, for instance, visual perspective-taking (e.g., staying in a room and fantasizing about what an individual from outside can see through the window). It connects up to complex mental challenges, for instance, assuming another person's guess about what a third individual accepts (e.g., "I believe Sarah still acknowledges that Frenkie does not admit what we purchased at Disneyland"). While increasingly noticeable eager compassion has a connection with progressively excellent emotions, increasingly compelling mental sympathy includes having continuously complete and exact data about another's substance, including how that individual thinks and behaves.

Right now, compassion, as despite everything, requires affectability and data about emotions. Regardless, abstract sympathy all around dismisses any reference to considering the other person, as required to be considering the opportunity of a type of Machiavellian cognitive empathy that can hurt other fellas. This thought refuses most if only one out of every odd single, conversational usage of the term.

The emotional part of it is associated with a cerebrum concept series, which is, comprehending that an individual's thinking pattern might differ from one's own. In an ordinarily growing kid, objective consideration of mind ascends between ages 3 and 5 (regardless of how essentials of this capacity, for instance, tailing another person's hope to reduce what he is staring at, show-off earlier). Theory of mind lacks one massive sign of mental irregularity, a cognitional issue that, for the most part, seems as it happens for the duration of regular day to day occurrence (other mental issues or cerebrum wounds can further convey empathetic insufficiencies). The way individuals accomplish mental compassion has conveyed some conversation. The multiplication sees estimates that individuals imagine themselves in other individuals' situations, a view that systems wonderfully with false accord impacts and other egocentric concerns packed in social mind examine. The theory sees fights that individuals make about human thought and then use it to envision and explain others' exercises, exposing individuals' ability to alter their perspective, talking to a specific another human.

An arrangement of methods has been made to evaluate empathy and its many other portions. Many of them are self-report dimensions (people genuinely rate how much they think they have slants comparing to empathy). Anyway, experts have similarly made innovative and dynamically target measures, specifically for evaluating empathic accuracy and clinical specialists' compassion for clients in treatment. Physiological measures and the coding of outward appearances are normally used to overview the active part of it. Lately, researchers have performed brain imaging methods to evaluate the cerebrum zones and promenades that are ordered when one is earnestly responding to the target person's endeavoring to address what that individual is going through mentally. These procedures have provoked theories about mirror neurons. These neurotransmitters (found in monkeys) respond in a comparative way when a movement is performed by self and when identical exercises are watched being performed by other persons.

Results in empathy consider contrast dependent upon which parts of compassion are being assessed. The examination of gender differences in compassion gives an example of the complexities of empathy: An inescapable sexual direction speculation exists that women are more empathic than the opposite gender. With this speculation, reliable results have been found when gathering self-report extents of empathic concern. The model is less clear while using target measures continuously, and gender differentiates are not found with extents of empathic accuracy besides under precise conditions.

Besides, the way that confirmation has been found for stable empathic properties in persons, compassion is perhaps better imagined as something that ascents up out of an unpredictable association between (a) attributes of the goal of compassion and its circumstance and (b) the attributes and motivation of the sympathetic, all introduced in a more significant social setting.

Overview

It is a comprehensive thought that implies the abstract and eager reactions of a person to another's watched behaviors. Having empathy improves the likelihood of assisting others and showing sympathy. "Compassion is a structure square of important quality for people to hold fast to the golden rule. It assists if they can visualize someone else's point of view." It is a fundamental component of productive associations since it supports us in grasping others' perspectives, demands, and point-of-view. Regardless of how they may seem, by all accounts, there is a sensible ability among sympathy and empathy to be relative. "Compassion is normally portrayed as experiencing another person's feelings and emotions by imagining oneself in that individual's condition: One fathom the other's situation as if he felt it. A capability is kept up among self and other individuals. On the other hand, sympathy incorporates the experience of being moved by or responding under another individual to grow after some time as a segment of human headway, which has a connection in the evolutionary period. Believe it or not, "Simple sorts of empathy have been found in our ancients, in puppies and even in rodents," a study purpose.

From a developmental point-of-view, individuals begin demonstrating compassion in socially organized efforts during very early vast stretches of life. According to an examination, "There is prompting verification that prosocial experiments, for instance, caring to create as it so appears in youth.

As energetic as a year mature, infant youngsters start to comfort losses of distress, and 14 to 18-month-old kid show unconstrained rehearses." While situational and biological effects shape a person's ability to comprehend, we look to have a relative level of empathy toward the span of our lives, with no age-related decline. As demonstrated by research, compassion was connected with a positive success and corporation profile.

Likewise, the realities affirm that we feel empathy due to the transformative piece of breathing space. Compassion, no doubt, progressed concerning the parental thought that depicts all warm-blooded animals. Hailing their state by smiling and crying, human infant youngsters urge their parents to make a move. According to a study, females who responded to their descendant's needs out reproduced the people who were cold and distant. This proposes we have a trademark tendency to growing compassion. Regardless, sub-cultural factors ardent sway where, how, and to whom it is conveyed.

It is something we make after some time and in relationship to our social condition. It ends up being a capricious response, which is hard to see its beginning stage in normal responses, such as energetic contamination.

In the field of mind sciences, empathy is the main focus. From a passionate health perspective, the people who have raised degrees of compassion will undoubtedly function admirably in the practical field, uncovering "greater gatherings of partners and all the more satisfying associations," as demonstrated by mental specialists.

It is fundamental in making productive social unions of different sorts, in the home, job, and other places. Nonappearance of compassion, therefore, is one indication of conditions like pulled back character and self-love issue. Moreover, for mental expansion specialists, for instance, authorities, having empathy toward clients is a noteworthy bit of effective treatment. Pros who are significantly caring can help people diagnose prior encounters and get an increasingly unmistakable perception of emotions and acts incorporating it. It expects a critical activity in the human, social, and joint mental effort during all life periods. In this way, the examination of compassion is a persistent zone of massive excitement for advisors and neuroscientists in various fields, with new research showing up routinely.

What is Empath Healing?

Compassion is the broad idea of practically an energetic experience; one is putting himself into others' shoes to sense their perspectives of life. This isn't empathy in having sorry or pity toward another, their feelings and circumstance. This is not empathetic either, an increasingly significant sentiment brimming with feeling sympathy that implies "to suffer" others' hardships and identify with inflicted pain. Having the alternative to identify remarkably three interrelated limits: to see and think about another's situation; to take another person's perspective through thinking-pattern and to feel as like the target person is feeling. All of these sorts of empathy taps the limit of "taking attitudes," that is, putting yourself inside another's seeing, whether or not it is in what that other individual sees and hears, thinks, and feels.

Portrayals now and again give increasingly conspicuous clearness. Seeing a parent at energetic last subtleties with an adolescent going around in a store or on accessible transportation, you may coolly and delicately say, "They sure are a bundle at that age, with such imperativeness to spend." You are busy with perceptual compassion by observing the situation the parent is going up against.

If you start a short conversation and the parent shares that their couple of tactics made their little youth effect, you may state, "I get how tedious it would be for you to acknowledge how quite far given what number of ways you've used with so little success to date." Here you are using mental empathy, that is, using your finding to put yourself into themselves.

Plus, you could state, "It feels there is a piece disturbing in recognizing your rising disappointment." In saying this, you tap brimming with feeling empathy by having the alternative to perceive and feel what the target person is going through. To the extent that all of these sorts of understanding are commonly exact and appreciated by the parent, more likely than not, the parent feels well-versed and supported in facing an inconvenient situation with their rowdy adolescent.

A couple of individuals can imagine what another is looking for and hearing any situation and remain with their own substantial experience. It is termed perceptual sympathy. Exactly when you can gaze and hear another's perspective, it can improve things enormously. A couple of individuals can move their thinking perspective and see another's point of view in the satisfactory partition to mentally generate another's exciting understanding while at the same time keeping their own viewpoint.

This is called emotional compassion. Imagine a parent grasping their youngster or young lady being so overwhelmed with extracurricular activities that their home-work and prosperity bears, all while so far collaborating on progressively worthwhile ways to deal with change their time and obligations and without repelling, enabling, or saying 'sorry' for them. A couple of individuals can recognize, sketch, and go through what the target person is feeling in a specific condition. This is called loaded with feeling sympathy when people cry in examining a book when they truly identify with a debilitated partner and feel their buddy's dejected, and when family members are chortling, upbeat and euphoric at the achievement of a family member.

Exactly when perceptual, scholarly, and loaded with feeling empathy are generally present, the provider and the given are one out of a common-looking and audience impression of the situation, taking the other's perspective and excited resonation. This is the point of fact one potential perception for making the term "grok" something to know in staying under and inside another's seeing of a condition, viewpoint, and energetic experience.

The attribute to use one's activity taking abilities to imagine another person's psychological point of view starts to developmentally be open and come corresponding after age five when the child will enough have the choice to imagine another person's perspective. A famous anthropologist stated it as "playing the activity of the other." It demands to step outside of one's legal avenue to see life from another lens. This sharp breaking point most consistently takes the three structures we are taking a glance at what the target person sees, thinks, and feels. Such activity may provoke sketching what another person, so observing, thinking, and going-through would presumably be inclined to do. The research found that when people are drawn nearer to imagine themselves in another's situation, they are less disposed to punish that person for their predicament and will undoubtedly respond with compassion. These researchers consolidate their disclosures: "Most likely distinguishing observers consider compassion the marginal response to undeserved wretchedness." Natural or human-made disasters and failures are remarkable to convey people's best qualities of offering themselves in significantly sober-minded help, noble purpose, thoughtfulness, and warm humanity.

Research talks about the troubles of sympathy inside couple associations as more a mistake of the inventive psyche than a failure of words. Past looking at the thinking and energetic portions of empathy, they notice the benefit of following a sympathetic response with direct dependability that conveys compassion. For example, when one associate feels stressed over the solicitations of home and child obligations and conveys how overwhelmed everything feels, the other accessory can offer a sympathetic response and show social assistance in supporting in dinner plan.

These studies similarly endorse that a couple feels sympathy to have it be commonly helpful. By keep going on with the example, later the stressed associate can discover over their mate's day and return a merciful response, for instance, "Since I've heard the day you had, I can see the constant issues you stood up to and that they were so difficult to manage and it torments me to see you being so shell-paralyzed from it." The line up directly with this thoughtful response may show up as offering the shell-staggered accessory some hot juice and a while later taking a walk together. Being vexed or centered around ourselves or being in the midst of a conflict can, without quite a bit of a stretch, square a caring response when a couple can postpone asking uncertainty points, search requests concerning where these feelings arise out of and what each expressly needs from the diverse as a merciful response.

"High perspective-taking" is likely to be typical for outstanding pioneers and compelling people working in occupations that demand significantly made civil tendencies, such as business visionaries and psychotherapists.

High limits in setting, taking consolidate the three pieces of decisively having the alternative to both appreciate and respond to life conditions, having the choice to see a situation from various angles, and seeing another's the point of view all around to expand a full perception of their thoughts. Right when we can truly get the unique truth of a related individual, we change ourselves to our shared humanness. To understand and travel through our misery, suffering, and distress is the fundamental portal to offer kind closeness and significant merciful resonation with another's torment, suffering, and trouble. This is to possess and experience certifiable sympathy. All else, including pity, empathy, mourn, and imagined compassion, may reflect the aching to be forgiving, yet we understand it is the ideal situation, a pale shadow.

Who Are Empathic Healers?

The unfortunate part of being emotionally sensitive person is that they're typically at risk of insecurity, 'people-pleasing,' victim mentality, or co-dependency. Once they have lived their entire life absorbing others' pain and suffering, without someone's knowledge to them, the subconscious tendency is to need to 'play nice' so that others like them, and so once they feel smart in their body, they'll feel smart in theirs. Moreover, whereas this might work typically, they tend to all bump into somebody sad, miserable or, faultfinding. An insecure empath can typically match the sad person's vibration, and as a result of once more, the subconscious belief is that to be 'liked' by somebody, they tend to should be like that somebody. From the attitude of being perpetually swamped by others' feelings, at first, to induce off from everybody, are precisely what empathy healers are. Through their dedication to healing work, the Universe aligns them with such a lot of varied healing techniques and practices that change them to measure totally and mirthfully in power as an Empath.

This confidence is vital. To begin learning intention on to existence rather riveting others' lower vibrations are a lot of centered and definitive in their belief, light, healing, and therefore the power of affection over-concern. They're radically amative, positive, and compassionate.

It does not mean responding to different people's unhappiness or negativity with a response that utterly dismisses the reality of their moment; that is, they are feeling frightened or upset.

It solely means rather than responding with validation or encouragement of others' negative outlook, and they respond with understanding, however conjointly complimentary support. In essence, rather than lowering themselves to satisfy them wherever they're at, they respond with the next vibration that forces them to rise to their frequency.

The best part is coming back to an area wherever they start to heal and unravel their own repressed emotions, and they start to embody such a high frequency that their minor presence is like a healing crystal for themselves. They now no more feel the need to be everything to everybody. The globe now not maybe a chilling and remarkable place wherever they feel unprotected from gripping the suffering and ill feelings of others. However, it becomes their consciousness playground wherever they get to observe taking the high road with others. Eventually, they begin to be happier, healthier, and feel many fulfilling interactions with others.

To better describe what an empathy healer is and what makes them a healer, an empath below-mentioned points describe them better.

Realization
The most significant shift occurs in life after they understand that they didn't have to be compelled to sacrifice their happiness for anyone else's. They understand that their feelings matter; however, they feel, their emotions and thoughts produce physical matters. They understand they have created several prophecies by taking in contrary feelings.

A time in their life is when they felt that caring for somebody meant essentially giving their last breath to them. They usually would neglect their feelings or desires to indicate the practice that others required them to. At some faith, they conjointly understand; however, usually, individuals mistook their real kindness as a weakness. They believe they will all conduct the flow and follow the trail of effort. They're aware that some relationships are inherently unequal. However, they've to let go of leading all the burden.

Remember feeling refreshed

When immersed in empath fatigue, dragging themselves through each moment will be troublesome to recollect what it sounds like to be bright-eyed and bushy-tailed. However, everybody has had times in their lives once they have felt a better level of energy. They recall those times, despite, however transient. Maybe it was a sense of pleasure over a forthcoming event that offered a burst of energy.

Possibly they recall a vacation at a peaceful location that allowed them some emotional period. The decision to mind, again and again, relieves them from the overwhelm. Dig deep into that memory and intensely feel; however, it felt to be relaxed and refreshed. They keep the peaceful smile on their face, the one that takes no effort and no muscles because it comes from deep among and fills their face. As they are doing this, their body responds to the memory as if it's occurring without delay. The escape in their mind reminds them that it's attainable to feel refreshed.

Make choices

They finally create choices once they are uninterested with all the emotional weight they have been carrying that vowed them to stop. They tell themselves, loudly and with pride, enough! Even as someone creating a new year's resolution, they felt a burst of energetic pride in this moment of clarity and call. Once they create this declaration, they use their thoughts to grant themselves a burst of energy. By their clarity, they gain a better energetic state. Creating a choice, they take hold of the approach they require to feel, offers a burst of energy they did not recognize was dormant among them. Merely creating a choice, any call, despite massive or tiny, offers them clarity that brings with it this vital energy.

Setting Clear Boundaries

They eventually learn to stay up for their betterment by stopping being a doormat. If somebody is not treating them well, they are saying in an exceedingly firm, neutral tone, "Let us discuss this after you are calm." I'd be glad if you stop." Saying no is an art. Empaths are usually I would aid to frustrate and pain others; however, it is vital to induce within the act of claiming that once things do not feel right. So they merely learn to say no; that seems to be a life-saving strategy for them.

It is a mind game

Feeling fatigued is all a state of mind that modifies rapidly. By practicing completely different methods daily, they slowly shift their state of mind and beliefs. They overcome their fatigue by merely changing their thoughts concerning people and situations.

They recall once they have felt healthy, gain clarity in their life, reach for the next frequency feeling, and appreciate each moment; they feel a touch of relief. By systematically doing this stuff, they notice a gradual shift in their everyday level of energy and should even realize enjoying the road to a better state of being. Instead of saying that I am continually tired or want an exact stage, they start these days by pivoting these thoughts to reality.

Vibrate higher

Fatigue comes from lower wave emotions. As empaths encircled by a world stuffed with stressed, bored, lonely, sad, and washed-out themselves, they become immersed in lower frequencies, dragging them down thus systematically to the purpose that it feels traditional. After they are in these low-frequency emotions, higher frequency emotions seem exhausting as they view them from an area of no energy. They acknowledge that joy, happiness, and excitement come to action, which sounds impossible after they are exhausted. The truth is that as they work for the emotional scale, their energy increases exponentially. They reach for higher frequency feelings even after they feel thus exhausted by shifting their thoughts ever slightly to attain an emotion entirely above their current state.

Reframing

This allows them to look at the experiences they are having from the upper self's attitude instead of the ego or the temperament. It helps them spot their own psychological feature biases and how they are connected to the story. After they produce stories regarding their experiences supported past encounters to limit their ability to be enlightened regarding the actual nature of reality.

Empaths are healers solely to the full extent that they perceive the flow of energy. They have a tendency to be acknowledged that no emotional or physical state is permanent. They tend not to carry these sufferings with them through life. Instead, empaths should permit themselves to unleash these negative emotions. Holding onto them out of guilt, feeling accountable, or unknowingness of their ability to unleash them solely blocks the flow of energy through them. They will perpetually absorb others' emotions, and however, once they are ready to acknowledge it and unleash it, they can relieve suffering and, in turn, relieve the suffering of others who are willing. They start experiencing life where they start feeling fresh daily and prepare to assist those in want. They let go of the energies that do not belong to them and permit the free flow that they tend to experience.

Why Do Empaths Suffer?

Empaths are not strangers to suffering; they naturally carry a significant load throughout the day. The empaths feel an intense level of unsteady emotions responding to things occurring around them. They soak up emotions outside of them and get a direction for daily fatigue. What makes this exhaustion worse is the inability to flee it. For the ordinary person, disbursement a while on the couch, reposeful to their favorite music, or a decent night's sleep is enough to make them feel relaxed. Except for the empath, there is very little escape. Riveting energy from objects, walls, the earth, or animals add to this overload of feeling. These empaths will feel like they need no choices for solitude. The main problem is that everything around them is energy, and empathizing plaguing this energy has very little or no escape.

Empaths are susceptible to people who are incredibly attuned to the emotions and energy of others. They combat the emotions of others as their own. This is a challenge after they have porous boundaries and find them fascinating about others' pain and stress. Empaths are sharply intuitive and are adept at reading individuals and things on the far side, only surface-level impressions. Because of their giving nature likewise as their keen insight into the human psyche, they are inclined to be natural healers.

As the day ends and empath crawls into bed, they hope for an emotional escape in their slumber, solely to enter an active dream state. Lucid dreams, vibrant colors, and vivid events of past, present, and future.

Uncontrollable whirlwinds of emotions reordering their mental and physical state while not acutely aware reprieve. Religious intruders, coming into the dream state and even luring them to entirely different places and out of body experiences. Empaths typically notice themselves awakening even additional exhausted, tensed, and stressed more than before they fell asleep. Being sensitive to emotions makes empaths caring, compassionate, and understanding of people. Friends and family tend to be their listening ear and a shoulder to cry on. Whereas most of the planet struggles to place themself in others' shoes, empaths possess real significant power, the power to see a person's perspective due to that they feel their emotions as their own. On the opposite hand, there are real challenges that go along with being therefore sympathetic. Empaths typically feel misunderstood to they feel, however, sincerely. They will additionally become swamped simply as they juggle the emotions they expertise from themselves.

Others' emotions flip their switch

It happens in no time. What truly happens that they are having an open day. Perhaps they got some smart feedback at work, checked off all the things on their disorder list, or were typically feeling smart concerning life.

Then, their partner gets home, or they converge with a disciple who had an awful day. Like a shot, they feel their emotions shift. Their smart vibes are no more there, and that they feel unhappy or angry, a bit like their friend or love. It feels as if their day happened to them. This makes it hard to carry house for the opposite person due to their currently attempting to manage similar feelings. As an empath, it is so difficult to disconnect somebody else's emotions from their own.

They perpetually battle emotional fatigue.
Feeling their emotions is exhausting enough. However, as an empath who picks up all of what everybody around them is feeling, it quickly becomes excessive. This includes sturdy emotions of any kind, from deep unhappiness to excitement and joy. Empaths must to strictly manage their emotions and practice much self-care to avoid exhaustion and emotional fatigue.

They struggle between going out and staying in.
Although empaths tend to attach well with others, ironically, they need some time alone to deal with their own emotions and have an opening from gripping others'. Generally, they are even mistaken for being introverts. If they do not have alone time, they will crumble below the pressure. On the opposite hand, maintaining healthy relationships is excellent for their mental state, and pure isolation is not.

It is a real struggle to balance alone time with a meeting. For this reason, empaths tend to like additional subdued settings, like occasional meet-ups at friends' homes, over strident clubs, or parties.

Alone time is essential — and not everybody understands that.
Speaking of needing time to recharge, it is hard to elucidate to others why they have it. For them, it is only time they'll properly hear them and type out the thoughts whirling around in their head. They additionally want quiet moments to "hear" and filtrate the emotions they will have picked up throughout the day from people.

Being an empath who lives with a partner or roommates or has extroverted friends, it's going to need long conversations to assist them in perceiving their solitary desires.

They struggle with anxiety or depression.

Although not true of each empath, it is not uncommon for them to struggle with their psychological state. As a result, they are sensitive to emotions their own enclosed; they will affect tons of diffidence, stress, and anxiety. Receiving anger or disappointment from others hit them with a large number of bricks. Empaths will feel the complete spectrum of mental and physical symptoms that accompany others' emotions together with depression, panic attacks, chronic fatigue, and more. This implies empaths may be left juggling the mental effects of their issues, yet as those of others.

Individual take advantage of them

Intuition may be a vast empath body politic. They typically have gut feelings once meeting new people who prove to be accurate, shielding themselves from dishonest individuals or those with ill intentions. Empaths do not seem to be resistant to deception, narcissism, and harmful individuals. It is necessary to observe out for those who try and profit from their sympathy, compassion, and temperament.

Small things deeply upset them.

They care tons regarding everything. It is only in their nature. So, like one mean comment from an unknown online or a disagreement with a coworker, tiny things will affect them for days and take an extended time to induce over. Others might not perceive why they cannot only recover from it.

Saying no is exhausting

"No" typically makes them feel guilty. Empaths hate dissatisfaction or paining others. Within the moment, they're happy to sacrifice their time or energy to create others feel lively until it leaves them exhausted and overwhelmed.

Sometimes they forget to leave emotional space for them

This is, in all probability, the largest current challenge empaths face. Once they're perpetually gripping emotional info from others, it is generous to understand what they're feeling from others vs. their thoughts and emotions. This could build choices, and generally, their "feelings" lead them down the wrong path.

Health issues

Being an empath is exhausting. There are health issues of being an empath too due to adrenal fatigue syndrome and sleep disorder. The largest con of being an empath is chronic fatigue syndrome. Once empaths are up to date with emotional people or people with countless negative energy, it will sap away at the empath's mind, resulting in severe debilitating energy. Negative emotions and painful thoughts cause a weakening of the system resulting in devastating results.

Most empaths have experienced lifespan with the emotional turbulence of people around them. They attempt to work out their personal growth and observe why they absorb disappointment, anger, fear, pain, and ache from others. However, all of this suffering comes right down to one construct that's an energetic imbalance.

They tend to experience the emotions of others through engaging emotional and physical energy. It's what makes them such extraordinary healers. However, it's also what ends up in their suffering and burnout if they don't perceive how to unleash this energy.

From there, keep operating high while not judging emotions; empaths get pleasure from hunting the stages in their mind, from blame to grief, to anger, up to happiness, and eventually actions. If they start to take it slow, get pleasure from any moment of improved feeling, and enjoy within the little uplift of energy. Simultaneously, not many steerages from those who perceive sympathetic talents leave to return to their conclusions concerning; however, they experience the world can help them reduce their suffering. Once they stop being uncomfortable, bad, confusing, or unknown, it helps elevate their negative energy and feel less guilt and sorrow for their inability to heal everybody utterly. Thus, instead of specializing in engaging and healing what they can and learning how to unleash that energy, they tend to move on, holding onto the negative energies that result in suffering to moving on, forgetting, and letting them help them to heal.

As a specialist and an Empath, I am captivated by how the marvel of empathy functions. I feel energetic that compassion is the medication the world needs at this moment. Empathy is the point at which we arrive at our souls out to other people and come at the situation from their perspective. The Dalai Lama says, "Compassion is the most valuable human quality." During these distressing occasions, it's anything but difficult to get overpowered by and universally. It empowers us to regard each other, regardless of whether we oppose this idea.

Compassion doesn't make you a nostalgic softy without wisdom. It permits you to keep your heart open to encourage resistance and comprehension. Being empathic may not generally be compelling in breaking through to individuals; however, I believe it's the most apparent opportunity we have for harmony in our own lives and on the planet.

It likewise takes exceptionally touchy individuals longer to slow down following a bustling day since their framework's capacity to progress from high incitement to quieting up is slower. Empaths share a profoundly delicate individual's affection for nature and calm situations. As empath's ability for profoundly created instinct and their inclination to be an intense wipe who ingests the world's pressure leaves them from somebody who is touchy to unnecessary tactile stimulation. Determining you're an empath will explain your requirements and which techniques to use to meet them. This is basic to increase a safe place in your life.

Picking compassion over anger and dread creates a significant move in our connections by and universally. It catalyzes an empathetic development of mankind and a desire for us to get along in increasingly important manners as people and as a planet. Empathy will be the main factor among war and harmony, disdain, and resilience. We have to become more significant than our little selves and consciences to be empathic in our lives. Compassion is a distinct advantage. The characteristic will eventually spare the world. Compassion stretches out a long way past a patient's clinical history, signs, and indications; it is more than a clinical determination and treatment. Mercy envelops an association and an understanding that incorporates the brain, body, and soul.

Communicating sympathy is exceptionally compelling and incredible. It constructs quiet trust, quiets nervousness, and improves well-being outcomes. Empathy is related to better adherence to prescriptions, diminished misbehavior cases, fewer missteps, and expanded patient fulfillment. When I initially viewed the video underneath, I was reminded, and overwhelmed, by the thought that the littlest articulations of compassion establish enormous enduring connections.

5 different ways: the way toward mending your injuries before you take any lashes for anybody around you

Disconnection
Detaching from the individuals around you, while hard for an Empath to do, is the ideal approach to begin the mending procedure. It is at the base of 5 things to follow. Escape, regardless of whether it is only for an hour or two. Try not to stress; the world will be here when you get back.

Acknowledgment
Try not to feel that you may be; acknowledge that you genuinely are. There is nothing amiss with you, and you are solely exceptional. The empath is a wonderful thing, yet they behold the broken. It's the remainder of the world that necessities to deal with you, not the reverse way around.

Claim It
When you have acknowledged that you are empathic, essentially, make it a piece of your identity – not a reason to feel how you do. Possess your reality, and be glad for what your identity is. It's assessed that every 1 out of 20 individuals is a genuine Empath—pride in your affectability to shield from feeling like a casualty of it.

Love It
Tolerating your empathic nature and owning it is significant; however, you need to cherish it most importantly. Once more, you are exceptional, one of a kind. Individuals throughout your life are honored to have you around. T

hat resembles a specialist reproaching his patients for being consumed. Being an Empath is only an aspect of what makes you what your identity is, not a condition to be dealt with.

Create Boundaries

At last, it is essential to build up limits. Consider your boundaries like a line in the sand. Leave it to the individuals throughout your life to remain on the other side of the frontier, and on the off chance, they cross it. Clear the air regarding your limits. Try not to make them undetectable. Perhaps the most challenging thing for an Empath to do is boot individuals out of their lives.

Why we need empathy healing

Empathy is a fascinating human feeling. It is a fundamental, base inclination requiring just a restricted comprehension to encounter. People can feel how others feel. When a companion meets the passing of a parent, you think some disheartening impacts also. It seems as though everybody's cerebrums are associated with this planet, helping us feel what each other feel and reinforcing our capacity to show empathy.

The explanation of compassion is fascinating. I have considered what empathy is and how it identifies with human cooperation, both old and current. I started to compose this to communicate my disappointment originating from my powerlessness to make sense of purpose; however, I wound up getting my very own smart thought opinions regarding the matter.

Sympathy is the thing that makes people prepared to do adequately connecting. It causes us to cooperate to fabricate a superior society for everybody, a feeling that cultivates the motivating force to encourage us to ensure and assist our neighbors. It's a little poke persuading people to overlook themselves, in any event for a minute, and focus on helping everyone around us. Sympathy might be the main thrust behind the creation and support of human advancements. On the off chance that individuals just paid special remembrances to themselves, it would merely be their most significant advantage to take assets at whatever point conceivable. This issue unquestionably exists; many people; in any event, reconsider before submitting an unethical follow-up.

Today, it is natural to lose the sentiment of compassion because of society's data move framework. How frequently do we hear a miserable tune on the radio, read a discouraging string on Team Liquid, or see many awful pictures on link news? TV, radio, phones, and the web has bombarded us with as much data as we need. My anxiety with this pattern is that it might be desensitizing us, not permitting us to use kindness to its fullest potential in regular day-to-day life.

When individuals were roaming, and a wild bear ate a kid individual from their gathering, individuals would feel for the individual. It was pitiful because somebody kicked the bucket, but since individuals were grieving the misfortune. On the off chance that another part had encountered a comparable circumstance, they would have a smart thought about what the guardians of the expired infant were experiencing. It was in that spot in their face, not a transcript or a story.

Individuals, despite everything, see and experience awful circumstances today. However, the over-burden of the events could represent the blurring intensity of sympathy. The more negative data we are presented with from our innovation frameworks, the higher the hazard of losing our remarkable sympathy.

There are likewise various sorts of empathy that an individual may understand:
Affective empathy includes the capacity to comprehend someone else's feelings and react suitably. Such passionate comprehension may prompt somebody to feel worried about someone else's prompt sentiments of individual pain.

Substantial empathy includes with kind truly experience that another feeling of individual response light that encountering. When feeling got humiliated and instance, they might begin to become flushed and disturbed stomach.

Subjective compassion includes having the option to comprehend someone else's psychological situation might think with light in circumstance. The therapist might identify the hypothesis of the mind and examine what others are thinking.

A different perspective of empathy to know before learning about the Empath

Explanation
People sometimes have childish, even barbarous conduct. The speedy output of any day by day paper rapidly uncovers various horrible, inexperienced, and terrible activities. The inquiry at that point is why don't we as a whole take part in such self-serving conduct frequently? Would it be that makes us sympathize with another's agony and react with consideration?

For this, some theories have been proposed:

Neuroscientific Explanations
Studies have demonstrated that particular regions of the cerebrum assume a job in compassion. Specialists have discovered that various minds' locales believe a significant position in sympathy, including the front cingulate cortex and the foremost insula.

Functional MRI additionally demonstrates that a territory of the cerebrum known as the mediocre frontal gyrus (IFG) assumes a primary job in the experience of sympathy. Studies have discovered that individuals who harm this territory of the mind experience perceived feelings through outward appearances.

Passionate Explanations

Some of the most punctual investigations into the theme focused on feeling what others feel permit an assortment of passionate encounters. The logician Adam Smith recommended that compassion permits us to encounter things that we may not feel complete. This can include feeling compassion for both genuine individuals and fanciful characters. Encountering sympathy for anecdotal characters, for instance, permits individuals to have a scope of intense encounters that may somehow be incomprehensible.

Prosaically Explanations

Humanist Herbert Spencer suggested that compassion served a versatile capacity and supported the endurance of the species. Sympathy prompts helping conduct, which benefits social connections. We are generally social animals. Things that guide our associations with others benefit us too.

Why People Lack Empathy

A couple of reasons why individuals some of the time needs empathy:

They succumb to psychological inclinations, at times, how individuals see various psychological predispositions impact their general surroundings. For instance, individuals regularly credit others' disappointments to inward qualities while accusing their deficiencies of external variables. These inclinations can make it hard to see all the elements that add to a circumstance and make it more uncertain that individuals will have the option to see a possibility from another's viewpoint.

Individuals will, in general, dehumanize casualties. Numerous others succumb to the snare of reasoning that individuals who are not quite the same as them likewise don't feel and carry on equivalent to what they do. This is most regular in situations when others are genuinely far off. When they watch reports of a calamity or struggle in an outside land, individuals may be more averse to feel sympathy if they imagine that the enduring individuals are on a fundamental level, not quite the same as they are.

Individuals will, in general, accuse casualties. Here and there, when someone else has endured a horrendous encounter, individuals tragically blame the loss for their conditions. This is the motivation behind why survivors of wrongdoings are regularly asked what they may have done another way to forestall the wrongdoing. This inclination comes from the need to accept that the world is a reasonable and simple place. Individuals need to accept that they get what they merit and merit what they get.

Influences
Not every person encounters sympathy in each circumstance. A few people might be more sympathetic.
The portion of various substances assume a job right now:

- In what way individuals see another person
- In what way individuals characteristic of another person's practices
- What individuals fault of another person individual's predicament

Past encounters, desires

Recent research has discovered that sexual orientation contrasts with practicing articulation of sympathy; despite all extract, these discoveries are blended to some degree. Ladies, in general, expect and feel more psychological empathy than men.

On the actual state, people give off an impression of being two primary aspects to add to the capacity to encounter empathy: hereditary qualities about being social. It comes underneath well-established commitments of support.

Guardians go lower qualities and add the general character, with an inclination toward people. Then again, individuals are additionally associated with folks, friends, and networks. Individuals perceive others in a regular impression about convictions, qualities which rained at an exceptionally young age.

Pros

The capacity to feel others' feelings is huge. Somebody feel on edge in a conference or out on the town, you can get on that and offer help.

If somebody encounters dread, you would have the option to see it and possibly help them either conquer their dread or escape a risky circumstance. It may even help you get mindful of a conceivably hazardous possibility quicker.

Likewise, you can identify with others in an unbelievably ground-breaking way. An Empath gives the truism "to comprehend what it resembles to stroll from someone else's point of view" entire diverse importance.

It's a force that should be appropriately taken care of. You can do it; there are fantastic endowments to acknowledge both for yourself and those you love.

As an Empath, your capacity to feel love and empathy for others is on an alternate level. Regularly, one of the most troublesome snags in a relationship is going to a shared comprehension. It requires some investment and extraordinary exertion to truly put yourself from another person's perspective.

As an Empath, you can't resist the urge to feel the full power of your accomplice's internal sentiments. This permits you to develop a degree of affection and empathy that is hard for others ever to achieve. This can assist you with improving your connections and better relate to other people, even those you'd, in any case, can't help contradicting. You comprehend others' feelings and discover shared views in a flash, developing great sympathy that moves you to act in a progressively kind and serene manner.

Cons
On the off chance that you know you're an Empath, you most likely observed this coming. Like the most different things in everyday life, here are the two positives and negatives to distinguish and legitimately experience the sentiments of others.

Legitimately encountering the feelings of everyone around you–without the capacity to single out what you feel–is conceivably hazardous and can be depleting, both emotionally and mentally, leaving you engaging with torment and disarray. Regardless of whether it's tension, despair, dread, stress, or distress, you're in that spot encountering it with the sufferer's direct without authority over it. Being an Empath can be troublesome under certain circumstances. The empath will, in general, be exceptionally delicate. This implies they have no channel for pushing back others' sentiments, yet they also become all the more handily overpowered by overwhelming clamors and occupied social conditions.

Combining these two things makes it regular for empathy to be vulnerable to freeze assaults and general sentiments of overpowering in occupied or rude conditions. For this equivalent explanation, viewing the news can be upsetting.

Once in life, we all need empathy healing to develop from depression and healthy life. We should seek the guidance of psychologists/psychiatrists to overcome empathy disorders.

The superpowers every empath possesses

All empaths are considered to be the most sensitive people in the entire world. They have some special qualities in them like they have huge hearts, which is not very common nowadays, they make strong relations, and can sense if something is wrong or something is not right, they can be spontaneous. Empath people are kind, sensitive, emotional, understanding, perceptive. The researchers found that the quantity of an empath in the world is not less, but the intriguing part is that meeting an empath is good or not because their attributes sometimes can be super annoying. They can sense people's intentions and emotions. Most of the people who are an empath do not know that they have these abilities that are different and unique.

Empaths have the following superpowers that make them unique:

Psychic Abilities:
Psychics are those who can read the minds, thoughts, and feelings of others. This world is super busy in their works, and they are not bothered anymore to get knowledge of essential things. Think about this attribute of an empath, and it will be fascinating to meet one because a psychic may answer those questions of yours that you have been asking yourself for many years. But having this ability is not something to have fun with, and it is not always an easy job. An excellent psychic has skills like patience, practice, and lots of self-love in them.

The world's perceptions about the psychics are some old movie characters with fog machines, their room is filled with crystal balls, the neon-lit storefront surrounds them, and people think that psychics have some manipulate supernatural occurrences. Still, the truth is that they are not that bad people make these perceptions about psychic because that's what they see in movies or cartoons. Most people think that this is the scams; psychics make assumptions about people on their own they do not have any ability or superpowers in them, but it is not true either. The ability of psychics is God gifted, something that is built in them. Many people believe in psychic powers because some events have been predicted, and they come true, but yet there are some events that they predict that went wrong. Empaths have the unique ability to assess a person's body language and emotions, and they can sense the wrong vibes surrounding them; sometimes, they can also feel the physical pain of anger or helpless person. These are the unique features of these people and are considered to be their superpowers.

Selfless:
Today many people in the world always think about themselves, and they do not care about others. There is a famous saying," If your love is only a will to possess, it does not love"- Thich Nhat Hanh. Selflessness is the best feature of human beings, and those who have this ability, their relationships can be unique in the world. But there are only a few people who have this. They don't live their life for selfish reasons like money, possessions, fame, prestige, and reputation; they prefer to live their lives with justice, happiness, or other people happy to help others is their main focus without caring about themselves.

Selfless people have the authority to let their selfishness out of their bodies. Their hearts and souls are pure, and they don't want anyone to be destroyed; they always think positively for themselves and others. People are interested in doing things that make them acquire more wealth, fame, ego, and powers; however, empath people always try to finish the darkness from others and always try to enlighten others. There is no doubt that they transform the world and make it a better place than before. That is their aim and goal in which they are very clear.

Sees people for what they are:

An empathic person has another superpower in them; they can see people who they are. Some people like only those who listen to them, these people want importance in their lives, but empathic people can see the reality of these kinds of people very easily. Empathic people always do what makes them happy, and they live their lives like they want to. They don't put any restrictions on them. One of the greatest abilities in them is that they can move on any situation; they don't fear losing unique people. They have discovered that they can find light and distribute it to others. They have this fine ability to see the truth into the people's hearts. Empathic people know better; they don't let fake anyone rule; they distribute light. They don't stay in the dark. One of them's best qualities is that they stay away from these kinds of people; they maintain their peace and happiness. They can see the true colors of fake people. They don't get manipulated. They don't let toxic people get into their lives to built toxic relationships because they know that they can destroy lives.

Seeing things that others may miss is the special ability of Empathic people, and they can easily observe people who are having a bad day, see the faults in people, and see rare potentials.

Positive Transforming Ability:
Empathic is also human they get angry, get sad, get overwhelmed, but the best thing about them is that they can transform the negative energy into positive energy. We can always choose to perceive things differently. You can focus on what's wrong in your life or focus on what's right.-Marianne Williamson. Empathic people can see reality, and they can make the reality of their own as well. We put the tag of good and wrong on things, and it depends on us. They know that changing negative thoughts to positive thoughts will make life happy and prosperous. They can change the pessimism into optimism. Empathic people change their negativity by being surrounded by positive people; they always make people who have positivity to transform their negativity into positivity because they are supportive and ready to do anything to make you happy.

They know how to embrace themselves. It is okay to look back and miss days that you liked but staying in your memories is not good because the time will never come back; all you have to do is to move. Sometimes you feel like you are no one in this world. You will regret that you gave your hundred percent to someone, but others betrayed. All empathic people leave yesterday in the past. They start striving for the future because they understand that no matter how bad things you faced, no matter how sorrowful conditions you have been through, there will be a time when you will feel lucky.

Sometimes you feel like you are the greatest ever born in this world, which is the superpower of an empathic person. They are very much aware of the negativity around them; they are very sensitive to pain, hardship, violence, etc. These affect them significantly. They don't neglect the fact that this world is full of negativity, and they don't get into depression or in a mentally ill state. Instead, they find ways to transform bad situations and make the world for themselves and others. They make people smile on a bad day, provide shelter for the homeless and others who need help.

Story of empaths

People have different kinds of perspectives, and everyone has their own unique stories. To understand the meaning of an empath, a lady who shared her story with us here name is 'Catherine Liggett.' She described that most of her client's work practices and tried to identify whether a person is intuitive or empathic. She has worked with many people and listened to many stories from empathic people. She met many people who can pick up the emotions, who are intuitive, and who understand the pain of others. After listening to many people's stories, she came up with the pattern, and she realized that there is an origin story like there is a tangible pattern for many people out there who are living their lives and facing empaths. She claims that she is very passionate about bringing more into the spiritual discourse. Empathy is a gift from mother nature, and this is a superpower of humankind. Still, this empathic ability is sometimes counted as a disability as well. Most of the people she helped them cope with their empathic nature because it prevents them from functioning in the world. For example, a lot of them cannot tolerate groups.

They cannot tolerate parties or at least not for very long, or they feel so drained in their lives or their significant relationships, and of course, they have to clear themselves daily. They have to have these rituals and these processes of self-healing to get through the day. Being an empath can also be a disability because it prevents us from the process of individuation, which is what Carl Jung would call the meaning of human life.

Individuation means that we grow to our fullest potential as a unique human being in this body on this planet in this lifetime and as an empath. It's very hard for us oftentimes to delineate where we begin, where our energy begins, and where that of another person begins and ends, and so if we cannot tell where we begin and end, how are we possibly going to tell what exactly we want from ourselves. How we carve our own unique path in the world, so here is the origin story she heard and shared with us. She heard this story over and over again from so many different clients who identify as empaths. We are often old souls who are born who choose to be born, if you will, into a family in which at least one of the parents, and usually it is the mother, does not have the support that she needs to thrive. As we are highly sensitive and attuned, we instinctively and unconsciously move into the caretaker role for that parent, and we never learn where our boundaries are, in other words. We never become our own person as our identity is hitched to being the caretaker for this parent. What that effectively does is we never accept that it is okay to have emotions that contradict. For example, if I am sensing that my mother needs my support, but this could also happen that she never asked for my help. I am possibly going to get angry because there are multiple things I want to conquer in my life, but it sometimes seems that life is not going the way I want to, which is completely fine, but the thing is why life is being so unfair to us. We are not able to live them according to ourselves.

Catherine Liggett claims that we have no connections to our power and our boundaries. In her work experience, she met a client who was incredibly empowering a reality and sense of self; she would just go around her reality and unconsciously sense what other people needed from her instead of being self-directed. Often something very tricky is as females in society are socialized anyway that our energy belongs to other people. Still, sometimes this becomes a very selfish thing to make ourselves before others to some extent. Yet, what is living for us because we are here to grow to explore things. We need to understand that life is not only about awakening, eating, and sleeping. Life can be more beautiful if you guys understand the true meaning of it.

She also said that there is another open dirty secret about the spiritual community and communities of healers. Empaths are the good healers because they are their comfort zone; why are these people so good at it. After all, this superpower is builtin in them. It is their childhood patterns. They have been doing this over and over again. Sometimes they are a little surprised because perhaps they are stuck in themselves; they are stagnant. If you are not intimate with this kind of community, you might put them up on a pedestal. It is because they are simply repeating, to be honest. Sometimes their energy seems depleted when working on their body language. Just intuitively, you might pick it up & it doesn't mean they aren't good at what they do.
She explored more she talked with a friend of hers who is also a professional the initiative. They talked about the idea that empathy is a disability, and she noticed that the more that she healed herself, the less empathic she became, in other words.

Empathic is more to speak useful to the people to drawback those empathic tentacles because someone needs help, so someone has to be there for that person, not just for taking advantage, to help.

Strategies for empaths to heal PTSD and Trauma

Empaths area unit usually was mistaken for being reserved or private. However, others don't notice that space you appear to stay in results from your target on protecting yourself and guaranteeing that the bottom is solid. This hypervigilance is very debilitating for empaths. Your past will still affect your present. Upon a disagreement with your partner, you will have an Associate in Nursing exaggerated emotional response due to your flashing back to the initial trauma.

Let yourself feel and categorize these emotions—a confirmatory expert will produce a secure surrounding for you. Learn to stay up for yourself. Conjointly bear in mind that "No" may be a complete sentence. Sensitive individual's area unit is usually afraid to bilk others; however, it's essential to urge within the habit of claiming "no" once one thing doesn't feel right.

Shower yourself amorously and kindly as you undergo the healing method. You're a caring one who deserves to be precious. Therein, you'll become comfortable along with your sympathetic talents and learn to shield your sensitivities from exploitation.

Empaths are at gamble for turning into hypervigilant, which is draining. You may also maintain a scanning think environment according to sure you are safe beyond being exhausted and getting into a state of hyperarousal. Suppose you were exposed to prolonged trauma and misbehavior as an empathic child, not intuition "seen" by thinner parents.

In that case, thou can also have ended up exquisitely attuned to your environment toward the faraway threat. When your younger fearful provision develops except healing, you may end up hypervigilant. Empaths are hourly wrong for snobbish. However, others don't recognize expectations because you're targeted about defending yourself, so the floor is solid. The Buddhists say, even is continually a groundless ground at that place to guide you. Even now, thou are submerged together with immoderate stimulation, and the groundless ground is continuously there.

7 Healing Strategies because of Empaths
1.Journal regarding thinner express traumas.
This is the advanced quarter to liberating yourself beyond the past.

2. Retrieve you inside the child.
In an exact moment, think returned according to when the prompt trauma occurred. How old have you been? Then picture yourself lager after the residence yet vile place. Tell the toddler, "I am sad thou have been hurt, or I desire certainly not permit that according to occur in conformity with you again." Then take the infant family together with greatness because of together with love.

3. Emotional Release. As thou heal, many thoughts wish surface: anger, fear, depression, self-doubt. Let yourself-sense or categorical these emotions—a supportive therapist can propagate an out of danger surroundings.

4. Set Clear Boundaries. Learn after rod up because of yourself. If anybody isn't treating thou well, impartial tone, "Let's talk about that when you're calmer. Also, remember as "No" is a whole sentence. Sensitive human beings are frightened in imitating disappointing others. However, it's essential to say "no" when something doesn't feel right.

5. Conscious Breathing. When your historical traumas are animal triggers, receive a little gradual extreme breath in conformity with tranquil.

6. Meditate. Regular recollection calms the mind, body, and soul; it decreases sensory overload and continues thinner law among a tranquil state.

7. Practice Self-Compassion. Shower yourself, including graciousness, as like ye go via the restoration process. You are a caring man or woman anybody deserves after lie loved. It is hourly to seek advice from a therapist in conformity with the action via the original trauma. As clearing trauma consists of EMDR, the Emotional Freedom tapping approach (EFT), and somatic awareness.

Reason1: Temperament: You'll be able to see it once they pop out of the uterus. They may tune in to lightweight, smells, touch, movement, temperature, and sound.
Reason2: Biological science: Sensitivity also can be genetically transmitted through families.
Reason 3: Trauma. It subsumes the same old healthy defenses that a toddler with nurturing folks develops.
Reason 4: Accessory Parenting. On the opposite hand, positive parenting will facilitate sensitive kids to develop and honor their gifts.

Folks are role models for all kids, particularly sensitive ones. "High vibes" are spiritually orgasmic to an empath. The World Health Organization is receptive enough. Past experiences of trauma (if any) don't build their predictions or insights; on the contrary, they create "readings. Empowered empaths learn to honor their talents and use them with confidence; they don't need validation from outside sources to follow their instincts. they're going for it. However, somebody intuitively senses that somebody is on the face of it kind and innocent – just for everybody else, years later, uncovering that their instincts were right.

Traumatic events make more significant the risk of depression, however in that place is also proof, so adversity performs leading to posttraumatic growth, including increased grace yet prosocial behavior. There is no experimental lookup pinpointing childhood trauma by increasing trait empathy in adulthood. Although incredibly counter-intuitive, it solely raises concern regarding after danger and renders the single more touchy to struggling, among others.

We explored this viable link using more than one study, self-report measures, and non-clinical samples. Further, the rapidity of the trauma correlated positively, including quite several elements of empathy. These findings endorse, so the trip about an infancy trauma will increase a person's potential to take the standpoint concerning every other. Future lookup needs in conformity with taking a postulate regarding performance measures and how its findings extend according to medical populations.

Tense occasions among childhood show psychosocial effects then organic levels about development in grown-up life. However, there is an abundance of research on the terrible impact of trauma. Emerging evidence suggests up to expectation experiencing vicissitude may additionally enlarge posttraumatic increase consisting of goodness then prosocial conduct. We tackle this hole of the composition by testing proviso trait empathy as adults, whoever experienced childhood trauma in contrast to those who did not. Trauma or maltreatment can also imitate various psychiatric stipulations, including borderline personality disorder (BDP), bipolar disorders, yet major depression. Childhood trauma includes unusual neuroanatomy within girls, or genetic associations, including infancy trauma and terrible outcomes. That has incursive behavior, yet BPD, in all likelihood, portion about the complicated causal hazard factors. A character may show extraordinary psychological modifications than non-public enhancements, resulting from learning received through coping along with the trauma.

Empathy is the potential in conformity with recognizing another's thoughts, along with a gorgeous intuition. Cognitive empathy is synonymous with principle concerning idea and 'mind-reading,' the capacity to the imitation of place oneself into any other person's shoes. To imagine their intellectual yet emotional states, then augur their conduct over these intellectual states' groundwork. Affective empathy is the pressure after every other person's intellectual states together with a fantastic effect. Sympathy is an exceptional action of affective empathy. That amount displays a person's response by the imminence concerning another to conform to deleting their judgment yet struggling.

There is a motive by assuming that empathy may circulate a position among the upshot on a stressful event. So treating trauma victims has been nearly no pilot assignment over the influence of the trauma of the victim's sympathy. Recent research using Lim, yet DE Steno suggests so much the celerity over last chance be the able government after multiplied kindness, and this hyperlink is mediated through empathy. It may be associated with expansion into prosocial then altruistic conduct. Hence, we hypothesized as empathy into maturity would stay rendered to stay excellent because of men and women, including an infancy trauma.

Given that empathy has more than one facet. Cognitional empathy is the capability after apprehending another's thoughts than feelings. Simultaneously, a passionate heart can respond in conformity with another person's intellectual state together with an appropriate sense. We performed twins studies. In Study 1, we requested adults by file salvo it had a history of babyhood trauma then according to whole an excuse about haul empathy, the Empathy Quotient (EQ). The unique 60-item EQ carries 20 gadgets, so are filler; hence we used the 40-item version in conformity with limit full participant fatigue. The EQ is a self-report dimension concerning each of the cognitional or passioned aspects over empathy.

Each over the ternary aspects consists of five gadgets. Cognitive Empathy includes: "I am excellent at predicting what someone pleasure feels"; "I will be able to decide between whether any individual else feels hastily or intuitively." Affective Empathy includes:

"I without a doubt revel in caring because other people"; and "I tend to get emotionally involved along with a friend's problems." Social Skills include: "I no longer tend in similarity with locating common situations confusing"; "I discover it sturdy in duplication of knowledge such as by slave between a neighborly situation."

PTSD is a reaction after a threatening event. Traumatic occasions might reason PTSD include observing a cherished one die, witnessing a Fervent act, rape, assault, then army combat. C-PTSD is more possibly by appearing than individual experiences a couple of then ongoing traumas or when a single trauma lasts because of a lengthy era. Survivors about concentration camps, humans who have been often abused as many children, and domestic onset survivors may trip C-PTSD. It may also involve military rank exposed after continuous violence, people who have experienced repeated sexual assaults, or kidnapping victims.

While PTSD usually causes disturbances, such as flashbacks, avoidance regarding locations, yet conditions remind an individual of the event, continual fear, and depression. This is because people exposed to extended trauma may also begin to digest the trauma as an interior part of their identity. They would possibly question their very own memories—believing, because of example, so perhaps the trauma didn't indeed happen.

SYMPTOMS OF COMPLEX PTSD C-PTSD has much over identical signs and symptoms, so PTSD includes intrusive recollections and flashbacks, depression, anxiety, avoidance, yet changes between personality.

However, humans with C-PTSD additional journey signs and symptoms, so humans with PTSD don't usually have. These include Chronic concerns of abandonment. Many humans with C-PTSD have a love disorder, then neediness, concern regarding abandonment, and regression at some stage when power is frequent into C-PTSD. They may have difficulty controlling thoughts and changes into a personality with disturbances of self-perception—obsession and the sinner. For example, a sexual misbehavior survivor would possibly suffice back then forth among viewing the abuser as sinister or loving or may continue a noxious entanglement together with that person.

Emotional flashbacks: Rather than intrusively remembering the traumatic event, a person with C-PTSD may get emotionally overflowing. They re-experience the emotions besides constantly, without a doubt recalling or questioning the stressful event. This is specifically common for the duration of intervals over stress. For example, a person might start sobbing then experience horror-struck throughout minor friction with his then her partner.

Treatment for complex PTSD Because C-PTSD is an enormously newly identified condition, there's nevertheless incomplete to remain treated. Exposure therapy, which is exceptionally high quality with PTSD, is well-read because of its usefulness in treating C-PTSD. Researchers typically advocated a stage-based therapy approach as includes the accordant phases:

Establishing security, then supporting the client to discover methods according to feel safe in his environment. They are teaching primary self-regulation skills, encouraging information processing that builds introspection. Strategies designed after limit distress yet make a more significant pleasing effect.

Plenty regarding particular period Empaths are often additionally touchy humans (HSPs) along with operative nervous systems, that means the front world executes crush to us easily. We also want time to contemplate and assume life; otherwise, we can experience flustered and unsettled.

We're human beings searching for excuses in imitating pressure single or frizz on into a calm area with a book. Peace is difficult to locate when surrounded by lousy people, sounds, or a range of stimuli. So, empaths want an ordinary singular era, then mini-breaks in refocusing, then recharge. It's no longer respecting being odd — it's about self-preservation then self-care.

1. **Routine disposition therapy**: Many empaths experience life around behavior or soaking of its healing qualities. It helps them drink a spoil beyond contemporary existence or be present with the natural splendor — such as a mild summer season breeze, drift water, and perky birds. Empaths aren't necessarily introverts, but similar to introverts, and they do tiny talk. Instead, they prosper among discussions regarding important, meaningful topics. When you're empathic, you assume deeply respecting the entirety going concerning it with a ball and then into your head.

2. **Limited period together with draining people**: You are aware of the kinds of people I'm speaking about. They're hourly referred to as "energy vampires" — those who seek because of the ball and leave ye affect sapped concerning junction or energy. Empaths hold significant hearts or need help to heal others. The trouble is we also bust regarding so much suffering, namely our own. When we stumble upon people, whosoever uses our empathy in imitation of their advantage, which may emerge as poisonous quickly. We need explicit boundaries along these boundaries. As that says, "No" is a perfect sentence!

3. **When within a relationship, empaths need partners whosoever understand**: While empaths are excellent in loving others, the solidity on a thick affinity can stand difficult. We do be effortlessly overloaded with the aid of our partner's energy or feel like we're dropping our period under decompressing. Empaths need imitation of a stand, including humans who apprehend that they are then okay redefining physical yet personal boundaries.

4. **Daily mindfulness practices**: Before my period starts, I can stay overloaded by thoughts and then feel so much in conformity with coping. Mindfulness is getting overseas regarding my tip yet calming my thinking or body. For some, mindfulness would possibly lie in everyday meditations. For others, that may lie journaling, flagrant breathing, then walks within nature.

5. **Peace then cools from strong noises.** The empaths can not hear their inner ideas in loud music, yelling, and sudden or repetitive sounds come frantically quickly. We want environments where we perform to hold clear moments often.

6. **The ability to receive (rather than always giving)** Empaths love to offer, especially now, we know its choice. We don't like sentiments like a burden, as can redact such challenging to receive assistance and then pray for support. But a balance of giving and taking is a share in healthy relationships — and disturbed health.

7. **Emotional release from previous traumas**: According to Dr. Judith Orloff, a psychiatrist and empath, both HSPs and empaths are partial in conformity with a range of varieties regarding post-traumatic stress. Because we feel the whole lot so deeply, we repeatedly develop up no longer knowing what to handle the sensory overload. Besides, we may ride bodily, warm abuse, neglect, bullying, familial chaos, and hold humans within our lives and didn't apprehend our touchy natures.

Effective ways to heal as an empath

Separate

Separating from those people who are surrounding you is very hard for an empath to do. This is the best method to start the remedial procedure. They should manage the time for themselves so they can better themselves.

Required Acceptance

This is something you are dealing with in daily life. It would help if you did not think about changing yourself. There is nothing erroneous with you, and you have a unique personality. The Empaths are an attractive thing, but most of them think there is something about their character wrecked. This is the responsibility of the people in the world to take care of you.

A person should Own It

When the person has recognized that they are empathic by nature, they should make it a part of who they are. This is not a reason to feel how you do; you should own your existence and be proud of who you are. It's projected that only a few people are a real empath. They should feel pride in their sensitivity as the only way to keep from sensitivity like its target.

Deliberate Extremely

The person can't pressure enough the status of consideration. There are factually hundreds of reflection techniques obtainable to study and perfect.

The person just has to discover what works for you and best for you. For some people, they need a specific type of music. Others need total peace. It would help if you took the time to figure out what works most acceptable for your brain. And how you would feel better.

Love It

For any person accepting their empathic nature and possessing it are important. Once more, you are very special and exceptional. Most of the people in your life are blessed to have you everywhere.

A person should Develop Boundaries

Lastly, it is dangerous to launch boundaries. This isn't a similar object as structure walls. A person should consider their limitations like a line in the shingle. So, leave it to the persons in your life to stay on their side of that line. When you know that they are crossing, it will be very much easier for you to maintain a distance. You should not make them invisible. It is also a tough one for an empath to do is wader people out of their breaths.

Not Essential to Take Concern for those People who are hurt

when you are an empath, you are excellently adjusted to other persons' discomfort, to adopt it as your own. You should always remember you can sincerely help other people. Well, you can attempt to assist them and guide them as much as you understand appropriate. Later on, the person feeling a unique pain must be eager to help themselves for any true curative. Often our kind natures shade us to the detail that many people don't want.

A person must have a concern about their pain
It a very significant step to repress your inner energy. When we are worried about absconding, suppressing, and avoiding our pain, we continue the cycle of our sorrow. Sit down and let yourself feel the exhaustion, the misperception, the annoyance, the upset. Once you face the discomfort, you think you develop to the next phase of hiring the sorrow to go.

You Are Not Insusceptible to Projecting Your Spirits onto Other
If we talk honestly, Part of the plea of classifying as an empath is that it occasionally delivers an entrance of seepage to us—a chance to pin others' responsibility. The person might immerse up the feelings of others like a loofah.

But it would not mean that you are excused from making. Well, it will all too informal to depict ourselves as wounded in life. This is much stiffer to take accountability for our contentment. A vital understanding of the path of remedial is to learn to differentiate what we are feeling from what another person is feeling.

Self-Esteem Plays a Big Role
Empaths with low self-esteem will hurt much more as compared to those with composed confidence. But not continually. Being an empath can be unclear, and it can be very informal to responsibility. The impossibility and insignificance we feel on the attack of incentives we knowledge each day. It will help us understand that the more sweetheart, admiration, and faith you grow in by hand, the less you hurt.

Shielding Is Not a Valuable Method

This is a provisional method, shielding can be obliging, but it is not a long-term answer. Shielding is basically about fighting air people's potency, and confrontation only helps to last the series of terror and pain within. Somewhat than aggressive, open yourself. A person should allow him to take time and practice to knowledge the emotions.

Empaths Intelligence Profound Feelings

Empathy is a sensation of another factual; an empath can tell the correct spirits that run profound than those depicted on the superficial. People usually put on a demonstration of look. This is a learned mannerism of beating true appearance in a progressively challenging civilization. An empath can intelligence the fact behind the shelter and act empathetically to assist that being fast herself. It will be making them feel at comfort and not so severely unaided. Empaths understand family, broods, friends, close connections, complete aliens, pets, plants, and lifeless objects; empathy is not detained by time and interplanetary. Some are empathic towards animals to the countryside, the terrestrial system, motorized plans or structures, etc. Others will have a mixture of the upstairs.

Empaths Consume Deep Intelligence of Knowing

Empaths are susceptible to telling one's aptitudes compassion to another's emotions and feelings. Empaths have a bottomless sense of meaning that escorts understanding and is often thoughtful and sympathetic. Characteristically, those who are empathic produce up with these propensities and do not study about them pending advancement in life.

How Empathy Works

Everything has a lively shaking and incidence, and an empath can intelligence these feelings and know even the changes untraceable to the bare eye or the five sanities.

They have a clear sense specific to the speaker. Behind that appearance is a control or force-field. Like hatred, often transports about a penetrating sensation that directly escorts the word. The word hatred becomes wired with the utterer's sense. It is that being's spirit energy that is chosen up by empaths. Whether the stories are verbal, believed, or just felt deprived of spoken and physical look.

Levels of the empath different psychic empathic traits how they heal

Psychometry - the empathic tend to obtain vigor, info, and imitations from substances, photographs, and chairs.

Mind-reading - the empathic aptitude to recite people's opinions

Mediumship - the empathic bent to feel the attendance and dynamism of feelings.

Physical Healing - the empathic tends to texture other people's bodily signs and often the aptitude to heal, convert, or transfigure them.

Emotional Medicinal - the empathic tend to feel another person's emotions.

Animal Communication - the empathic aptitude to hear, texture, and connect with creatures.

Nature - the empathic aptitude to feel and connect with the countryside and with vegetations

Geomancy - the empathic aptitude for reading the vigor of seats and the terrestrial - geomancers can feel the dynamism of the Soil, such as Grassland lines. They can also get annoyances, discomfort, or nervousness before tremors and other tragedies happen wherever on the earth.

Premonition - the empathic aptitude to feel when approximately something is about to happen.

Knowing - the empathic capability to texture what wants to be done in any given condition, often escorted by a sensation of calm, smoothness in the middle of a disaster.

Psychic empathic traits include the aptitude to obtain energy and comprise the facility to heal in numerous cases.

For this reason, an empath's life trail is the slightest right to the healing arts. Whether it is in the arena of healthcare or therapy or working with broods, vegetations, animals, or even curative places, finished design, and face-lift. There are many different tracks for developing an empathic vigor healer - you just need to control which characteristics and statures of an empath resonate with you most. Once you have an optimistic opening for the psychic aptitudes of being empathic, you can get information harmony and contentment. This lets you overwhelm the irresistible feelings of why an empath textures nervousness. The remedy can oblige anyone to reach a concord state, but what is even more significant for those with mental empathic characters is to support ongoing substance and resistance. You must envisage by hand enclosed by a fizz or ample white light that protects you from external energies. When you are very sensitive, you may want to upsurge these defense limits by visualization multicolored coatings around you.

It is also significant to imagine yourself beached and linked to the soil so you can remain stable, stable, and secure. It is obliging to use the assertion. A person should always remember that those with mental empathic characters are talented enough to obtain and pick up vigor. But they can also scheme curative energy.

One of the best and easy ways to develop an empathic vigor naturopath is merely using your meaning. When you obtain feelings from others, or smooth from the entire world, you can opposite the schism and send out curative energy. It would assist if you closed your eyes and envisage a massive sun overhead; you distribute an unhappy ray of light into your emotion and down into your hands. This is what will give you concord. The upcoming is not set in stone, and we are not wounded. We have the talent of free will and the control to alteration, so we must not be frightened, even when it appears irresistible. Empaths are silent highfliers but animated in areas of emotional joining. They find that speaking about expressive subjects is a great opening that aids in sympathetic actions. Some empaths can conflict with empathy since they are overcome or powerless to grip feeling. They can be absorbed external to what others feel, somewhat than themselves. This is a shared trait to numerous people who have not gone finished a procedure of self-development. They avoid conflict caused by expressively stormy situations. This caring of state can effortlessly make a painful feeling since empath textures this feeling. Empaths are sensitive to brash noise and television. Television agendas portray emotional drama like the newscast and forces shows. They struggle to understand the performances of unkindness and corruption that involves sad others.

They struggle to understand sorrow in the world and are often romantics. They are animated, so they can frequently be found in parts of the melody or the paintings. They frequently consume the aptitude to attract others to them. This comprises broods and animals as they have a balminess and sympathy that is beyond usual. They can be very good listeners because they usually have an interest in other people or temperamental broad disposition swipes due to irresistible thoughts, spirits, and feeling. They are likely to have additional supernatural pieces of knowledge in their life. This could be a stellar forecast, mental aptitude, or diversity of other pieces of knowledge. Empaths are idealists that have trouble keeping absorbed. This is shared with people who deal more with feelings and neglect. Like many people on a mystical path, Empaths often experience and synchronicities. This is somewhat that happens to everybody though empaths are frequently more conscious and, therefore, look out for it.

Empath medicine

Emotional Empath
The emotional empath is the excellent shared kind of empaths. When you are this type, you will get effortlessly choose up others' feelings about you and feel the belongings of those feelings as if they were yours. The expressive empath will intensely knowledge the spirits of others in their expressive body. For emotional empaths, it is noteworthy to study amongst your spirits and peoples of others. In this way, you can use your aptitude to assist others deprived of flattering exhaustion.

Plant Empath
If you are a plant empath, you instinctively know what plants require. You will be green-fingered and have a factual gift for inserting the correct vegetable in the right home. Many vegetable empaths choose to work in gardens, parks, and rough sceneries where they can put their aids to good use. In detail, when your job comprises plants, then you are maybe a vegetable empath. Some people with this gift receive leadership from trees or plants directly by hearing it.

When you are this caring of an empath, you will previously know that you interact with vegetations and vegetations. You might like to reinforce this bond by sedentary silently by a singular tree or plant and adjusting additional care to its wants and leadership.

Animal Empath

Most of the empaths have a strong connection with animals. Though, an animal empath will perhaps dedicate their lives to upkeep animals. Those with this gift will distinguish what an animal wants and maybe talented to psychically connect with the being. When it comes to an animal empath, you spend enough time with animals; studying animal psychology or biology helps you refine your gift. It can also be considered to take training as an animal healer as your special talent can make you able to find out what is wrong with an animal & treat it accordingly.

Intuitive Empath

When you are a natural empath, you will choose up data from other people just by being around them. Your willpower directly knows when somebody is dishonest to you since you can sense their arguments behindhand. Those with this gift reverberate to other active fields and read the strength of others very effortlessly.

When you have this attitude, you need to border yourself with people with who you feel allied. With this gift, you might need to reinforce your active field so that you are not continually bombed with others' opinions and feelings.

It is challenging to empathize; it may be disorientating, confusing, and exhausting to you. However, understanding the types of an empath can help in using your gifts & those around you.

Empath self-care

Listen to Your Body

A person should always learn how to listen and care for their body.

They should not wait for someone else; your body's exhaustion, mind's misperception, gives you out enormous naught on how a person is treating themselves and their body.

Live in The Moment

A person should avoid worrying over the past and about tomorrow. Focus on one instant at a time, one day at a time, and one task.

Nurture Your Body

A person should learn how to love and cultivate your body, just like you would grow, love, and care for a youngster. You merit to be precious and be concerned about the way you care for others.

Feed Your Body

A person should give their body the accurate fuel, always the right liquid, the proper nutrients. They should avoid satisfying it with quick-fix successes of caffeine, honey, food that pressure out your dominant anxious system.

Learn to Meditate

Learn how to observe. Thought will help you slow down and help you develop more conscious when you're hitting others' needs before your needs.

Learn to Relax

They should learn how to reduce nervous and harassed feelings correctly. You will discover it problematic to change off. So, rest and reduction will energize your body. Good superiority, sleep is essential for the physique to heal so that the person would feel refreshed.

Listen to Your Inner Guidance

You should take the time daily to attend to your inner guidance. When a person is extremely busy, nervous, and stressed. You cannot catch your internal voice. You are frequently too eventful attending to your terror, your personality.

What is negative energy to empathize with?

Who is an empath?
An Empath is someone with a powerful ability to sense other people's feelings, emotions, and energy. Often it is unbearable to the point, but it doesn't have to be that way. It can be controlled to accept this privilege and even enjoy it.

What is Empathy?
Empathy is the ability to understand and co-experience other people's emotions and thoughts. It doesn't only help develop and maintain good and stable relationships but also function more efficiently and ultimately achieve more success in life.

Empathy is crucial because it allows us to consider how others feel to react to the situation appropriately. It's usually correlated with social interaction, and there's plenty of evidence suggesting that increased empathy contributes to more behavioral support.

What happens when you realize you are an empath?
It's like removing a blindfold from your eyes. All of a sudden, things start making a lot more meaning. In the context of your very distinct personality style, your perceptions, emotions, feelings, and relationships with other people can be seen and understood. You've had to face tags for your whole life; you may have been labeled sensitive, frail, or even disturbed. You have now found a mark that suits you, and that makes you feel good about it. You have a newfound personality, an improved sense of self, and a conviction that you can now start discovering your inner and outer workings with greater trust and experience.

The moment you learn that you're an empath, you know you're not alone. You've joined a group of other people out of the blue that shares your ability. You're well filled with the sense of togetherness–something you've rarely experienced up to this level. Although individuals feel compassion for others, empathy will take on others' weight as though it were their own.

What happens when Empathy exceeds limits?

Becoming extremely empathetic means you are much more likely to be influenced by negative energy and positive energy from others. To be an "absorber" of other individuals' feelings and energy can have an emotional, physical, and spiritual effect. Recall the last time you fought with others, and you feel exhausted entirely. Just imagine that you already feel physically exhausted, without even making an argument, simply by being in the same room as another individual.

While we need to offer emotional support to the ones we love, we need to shield our hearts from those who reap the benefits of our generosity.

Many who live in a negative mental set appear to vibrate at low frequencies. Their energy will become toxic to the Empath. Since many Empaths find it challenging to be around this form of force, they may need to detach from them or stop spending time.

How does empathy become a bad trait?
For example, a particular fellow (the one who thinks and therefore sends harmful thoughts) shows up regularly in mind, along with negatively charged emotions, during the day or nights. Yet you wrongly believe that it is your problems that generate angry thoughts. Empaths are susceptible to people who are highly attuned to other people's emotions and resources. They can easily take other people's feelings on as their own. This can be a problem if they have weak barriers, and they will end up absorbing other people's pain and tension. Empaths are highly natural and capable of reading people and circumstances beyond mere practices at the surface stage.

An empath or an emotional sponge?
Empaths may become confused emotional sponges unless they are vigilant, swallowing anger, or toxic guilt, which is not theirs to bear. Empathy interactions can result in satisfying healing on both sides–or they can end in empathy fatigue if it is without appropriate limits. The darkness of this skill is that while empaths bear tremendous power to assist in recovery, they also fail to heal themselves in the course.

Not all Empaths are "light and happy," Far from it. Some suffer from depression, anxiety, multiple addictions, and self-doubt because of their high vulnerability and receptivity to take on other people's emotions. The strength of the perception witnessed by an empath will easily leave them exhausted. Their feelings are part of a complex network of their own experiences, other people's expectations, responses, and feelings around them.

It is completely fine to own yourself:
Most significantly, empaths must understand that it is ok for them to own their shadows. The darkest parts of themselves offer valuable insight into successfully incorporating various phases of themselves to become complete.

It doesn't mean giving into the darkness, but utilizing it to generate more energy in the world. Repression leads only to more distress—however, getting these physical symptoms to the surface gives them a better chance of access to medical care and healing.

To these deep and extreme levels, the reason why many empathize is that they perceive and sense other people's feelings as if they were theirs. It can be part of the curse side of the "empathy blessing and curse" because experiencing other people's emotions and thoughts can be incredibly unpleasant and traumatic.

The negative energies:
All things like emotions of fear, rage, frustration, and stillness are energies. Unfortunately, you can actually' pick up' or absorb such energies from other individuals without knowing it. When you are an emotional sponge, learning how to stop taking negative feelings is essential.

The bad news regarding negative emotions is that breaking down your defenses, chronic anxiety, depression, or stress will turn you into an emotional sponge! If these emotions' strength is weak, the internal strength will significantly reduce.

Empath skills are a blessing for the rest of the world. There are two sides to the coin. However, it could turn out incredibly hard for the empaths to hold the dark side of their powers.

On the one side, empathic abilities make other people feel comfortable while they're in the company of an empath, and as a result, empathy is the one that creates the strongest bonds with others. Nonetheless, on the other side comes the tension that empathies have to deal with when coping with other individuals' feelings.

The face behind the mask of an empath:
The dark side to being an empath comes in the form of two conflicting powers residing in the mind of an empath.
Empaths will still sense both the positive and the negative. In the heart of an empath, the negative and the good work together. And normally, empaths will feel confused by one or the other. These individuals, however, are much more prone to negativity.

Their good knowledge of the dark side of life makes them susceptible to the world's toxicity.
Their deep understanding of the processes of life and people's relationships also makes them feel overwhelmed by others' feelings. What disturbs them the most is harmful energy. As they are natural healers, they still want to relieve others' suffering and therefore make it their own.

Empaths constantly consume those energies. Empaths are often drained or at least tired from emotion.
Yet they're never telling the world anything. They just listen and feel. And would deliberately neglect both their body's and mind's needs to relieve others' suffering.

The negligence, however, builds up over the years. And, it eventually contributes to a need for empathy to restore their spirit.

Once an empath falls in love, they will never dedicate themselves to the one they love.
They still can not let go of all the misery in their hearts that they have collected. And, if they do, their affection for both spouses may be too intense and very hard to manage. That's why they'd keep a bit of it away from the rest of the world. They are holding a guard up because they need to.

The inner struggles are another dark aspect of being an empath.
Empathy exists in a perpetual struggle between sorrow, misery, and goodness. And they would always be overwhelmed by their sad side and will contribute to self-destruction. The only way to fight this war for an empath is by admitting that they can differentiate between their emotions and their overwhelming energies. Empaths ought to heed their feelings and make them a priority.

The dark side of empaths is challenging to bear. By holding others ' sad feelings in their heads, empaths often seem to neglect their own needs and continue to bear the others' weight on their selfless shoulders for their entire lives. Empaths should recognize that it is not their duty to deal with other people's problems. If you want to prevent the dark side of empathy from consuming their lives, an empath shouldn't owe every person they encounter. They can also break the barriers that surround their heart to enable their empathic self to do better in their own life.

How do empaths release negative energies?

Any negative feeling can come from several sources: everything you feel can be your own, it can be someone else's, or it can be a mix. Most people have empathy, but to some degree, everyone has the potential to be empathic, too–it may just take practice, and they can just feel the emotion in people they are close to, but everyone can practice it!

If you're an empath, you appear to sense other feelings, emotions, and even physical suffering. You can also carry on this physical suffering without realizing it, depending on the degree of your empathic abilities. This is why energy perception and grounding are central elements of energy clearing.

What are the types of empaths?
1. **Emotional empaths:** who takes on other people's feelings and sentiments
2. **Physical empaths**: takes on the body's energy
3. **Geomantic empaths:** environmentally friendly who pick up energy from another region
4. **Plant empaths**: who knows about the requirements of the plants.
5. **Animal empaths:** ones who know about the needs of the animals
6. **Intuitive empaths:** which takes things up just being around individuals
7. **Old Soul empath:** who sees the positive in everyone, no matter what, and still tries to repair people.

8. **Unaware empath:** who don't realize that he is an empath

Ways of how empaths can release negative energies:
Sensitivity is a blessing. You can feel other people's energies does not mean that you are frail or defective; it does mean you are free, complimentary, and different! It also means you have a real need to learn how to release negative or unnecessary energy so that you can feel lighter, healthier, and happier.

Meditation.
All empathy is required at some stage to absorb the frustration, negativity, and suffering of others. Another quick meditation for five minutes will help them release extra energy. Again, find a quiet, relaxed place to sit down, test posture, and start deep breathing to calm yourself.

Cut the Strings
It is a very critical job for which an empath has to become very professional. Since you are so good at making friends and people love you, they may take away your happiness from you because your satisfaction feels so good, soothing, and caring. It happens because you unknowingly permitted it.

Past and current ties may still exist with family members, relatives, and partners, long after the connection is over. It's time for cutting the cord! Imagine if the individual you had a relationship with and see the cord is broken to cut ties.

They are clearing you the cloud of negative thoughts.
Your mental body is actively communicating with others, and you pick up on other people's negative thoughts.

You build your thoughts, as well. Be aware of the following kinds of thinking: Negative, Repetitive, Constant, and Automatic.

Your job is to check in several times during the day if you feel anxious and stressed, see if you have picked up or produced some negative thought-form, and actively let go of it.

Using mind mapping, drawing, and painting
Empaths seem to be very creative and enjoy when they feel amazing, expressing their talent. They prefer to suppress their creative ability when they don't feel great because art requires them to deal with their emotions, causing pain. Try using it as a means of emotional release and healing to support you when you feel trapped and out of control.

Cry to release your emotions.
Empaths have an emotional body that is very refined, and they like to weep when they need to. Crying has many advantages in healing. The crying sensation acts as a soothing tool for your aura. This is what kids do all the time. Another way of keeping your aura healthy and in alignment with your soul's course is to do the energy work.

Visualization to Shield
Shielding provides a simple way to secure yourself. The second you realize that you're uneasy with a person, location, or situation, secure yourself with a shield. Take some long, deep breaths. Then imagine a stunning white or pink light shield that completely covers your body.

This shield will secure you from everything negative, stressful, or disruptive. Inside this shield's defense, feel centric, relaxed, and energized. This protection removes negativity so you can always hear what's good.

Linking oneself to nature:
Nature is the best healing energy source for someone who feels overwhelmed by emotional tension and mental trauma. Humans bear the most realistic feelings and negative emotions. And if you're empathic, go and spend time alone in nature to refresh at least once a day. You'll let nature clean you up.

The most calming energy healing therapy you can get is communicating with plants, trees, water streams, and natural landscapes. And it's completely free of charge!

Sit on the ground against the trunk of a tree with your back, or walk bare feet to draw positive energies from the earth. The earthing or grounding will make you feel very good.

Massage.
There would be no full list of simple ways to release excess energy without relaxation and efficient stress-relieving therapy. "Put away any thoughts that massage is either an excellent way to treat yourself. Massage may be a powerful tool to support you in taking responsibility for your health and well-being, whether you have a serious health problem or just looking for another stress reliever. It is also possible to learn how to do self-massage.

Salt.

Salt is one of the most time-tested and readily accessible methods of curing yourself of toxic energies. Salt energy clearing methods include salt baths, sprinkling salt in a circle around you, or some other choices.

Next to the sea, or a pit of saltwater? Take a bath and imagine the negative energy that washes away from you.

Another way to cleanse with salt is a neti pot, which is especially helpful in removing negative thoughts and memories. Because it cleanses the nose, mouth, sinus passages, and the third eye, using a neti pot with salt helps to release memories of falsehoods spoken or behaved against you.

High Vibration Music.

If they're drum beats, pop melodies, or singing bowls, high vibration sounds are the easiest ways to get rid of negativity. This emotional cleanser will change the attitude immediately because of the music's inherent ability to overcome the ego.

Crystals.

Earth is filled with gems–as shown by Mother Earth's fantastic storehouse of crystals. Some crystals are also excellent eliminators of toxic energy along with acting as decorative items and jewelry. Look for Black Obsidian, Rocket, Lava Rock, and Black Tourmaline when it comes to removing "evil vibes" from yourself or your house.

Often suitable for clearing are smokey quartz and selenite. Additionally, Green Calcite and Serpentine have releasing effects. If your goal is to deflect harmful energy until you consume it, your best bet is Hematite or Labradorite.

Reiki.

Reiki is not a massage but a religious practice. Reiki is a frequency of energy that eliminates emotional obstructions. Negative energy is always stuck (obstructed energy) when it comes into contact with Reiki, which releases it. With thousands of clinics, spas, and private practitioners now offering Reiki, localizing has also become more comfortable.

Aromatherapy.

If lemongrass, clary sage, or cedarwood is your preference, these days, essential oils are all the rage! Our ancestors understood herbs and plants' ability to heal and cure several problems with roots dating back thousands of years.

Prevent overloading Empathy

When feeling other people's discomfort or symptoms and releasing the toxic energy, inhalation of natural lavender oil or placing a few drops of it between your eyebrows can help you calm down. You spend time in nature when you can. Combine your time alone with time for friends. Set firm limits for energy vampires and people who are negative. You don't have to justify yourself anymore.

These are some steps the Empaths can adapt to and release the negative energies and feel better.

Become A Healer Instead Of Absorbing Negative Energy

Recognize Yourself As A Healer

Our universe runs on floods of unlimited energies. Everything that we see, do, or feel makes energies around us. Individuals who are sensitive or are empathic can detect these energies. The recognition of your capabilities is essential, whether you have the abilities of a healer or not. On various occasions, we question ourselves or feel that something is going on out of a single incident. In all reality, we neglect to perceive that we are likely more intuitive than others.

Here Are Ways To Find Out Whether You Have Healing Capabilities Or Not.

1. You Do Not Dreams; You Have Ideas:

Your dreams have connections, and you see them since they are associated with your life. It is not only an incident. Your inherent energy can detect the power of something you will look at later on; this recognition of energy shows in your visions, and it turns into a dream.

2. You 'know' Things Before They Happen :

You do not have to dream consistently to see the future, but it may occur in the future. Since you empathize with high instincts, understanding this universe's energies is your strong point. Associating with these energies provides you the warnings.

3. You Know Whether The Other Individual Is Lying:

You can quickly catch others lying not by their words; however, their frequencies never need proof to see a liar by their signals. Regardless of knowing the reality that the other individual is lying, you do not generally reveal it.

4. You Have Connections Just With A Couple Of Individuals:

You converse with many individuals but have a soul connection with only some of them. They know and understand you for quite a while. You would not become close to any individual who gives negative energies. You are generally alright with the ones with whom you feel this bond.

5. Individuals Come To You For Mental Harmony:

People come to you to solve their issues. Regardless of whether you cannot solve their problems, they feel better after speaking with you, spending time with you. They get support from your positive energy.

6. You Look For Isolation Frequently To Energize Yourself:

You have to recharge yourself a ton, and you can do that. By spending time with yourself, you can renew your internal strengths so you can go out, forbearing the world. If that you are a profoundly natural empath, feel honored to be one. Deal with yourself while you are dealing with the universe.

How To Become A Healer

Every single person absorbs and radiates energy, purposely or accidentally.

We have empathic inclinations in us. A few of us know it. This legitimizes the uneasiness, the distress, the confusion, and the combination of blended feelings we face while talking with somebody.

A few of us have protected ourselves from these vibrations, while the enthusiastically touchy empaths have let themselves get influenced by this world. Being an empath accompanies both positive and negative sides.

The benefit of being an empath is recognizing the exact type of energy inside others and can pass judgment on an individual without evidence. They can not just understand others, and they can likewise heal both themselves and the world. The view of being an empath is falling into a condition of confusion. With an excessive number of energies around them, they can get confused.

Almost in every case, there are specific approaches to start managing the darker side. As an empath, you have to use your healing potential not to hurt yourself during the time healing the world.

Here are five different ways you can do this:
1. Be Confident:
The minute you begin creating your vibration on the universe, you start emitting your recurrence instead of getting to make a huge distinction. To do this, you need certainty and faith in yourself. Be confident about what you do.

2. Do Not Be Insecure:

Ambiguity is one of the significant obstacles which keep you from turning into a healer. You do not have to satisfy everybody. If they do not care for you, there is no motivation to concentrate on them. You may be distant from everyone else when you can manage everything. If you rely upon others, you lose your confidence. In our feeling, we tend to regard everybody as independent of what sort of individuals they are, with the intent to consider us. We all are not the equivalent. Individuals with negative energies will never respond to great ones.

3. Be hopeful; Convert Others' Pessimism Into Optimism:

Irresponsible Empaths easily get hauled into negative feelings of others. They absorb these feelings to feel the suffering. Rather than occupying the agony, they should understand it and point out its positive sides. If that something is not going right, that suggests there are some other options. Discover the positive parts of everything. It won't just cause you to feel great yet also heal the other individual as well.

4. Help Other People Discover Their Positive Sides:

While it is significant for you to adore yourself, it is likewise vital that you make others love themselves as well. That is how you can heal them. Show them their positive sides, their abilities; cause them to feel great about themselves to transmit positive energy and figure out how to be visionary.

5. Remain Quiet And Calm:

Try not to go crazy despite how distressing the circumstance is.

Irrespective of whether somebody pulls you in a zone of pressure, recall that you can heal everything. Try not to respond since this will make negative vibrations in a tough situation. It isn't so hard to turn into a healer. You should concentrate on yourself and the energy of this universe.

The negative influences of some people affect us, and the social events frequently become excruciating for us.
In any case, we should not escape from them. Rather than passing up the enjoyment and happiness, we ought to be there for social occasions and get ready for the goal that these people's grief does not influence us.

Impact Of Negative Energies On You
There is a wide range of effects on our feelings that can positively or negatively impact our lives. The more significant part of us has caught wind of positive energy and can assist with prodding us on and giving us a more brilliant standpoint. Be that as it may, there is additionally the flipside of the coin to consider: the opposing side.

When negative energies surround you, your state of mind, feelings, and sentiments would all be able to be antagonistically influenced.

However, a few people experience a clairvoyant assault, decline to analyze it, and attempt to push it to the back of their personalities since they feel that no one will trust them. In any case, there are different signs to pay extraordinary attention to.

A Few Of The Common Signs And Their Effects

1. **Feeling Tired And Afterward, Sleepy:**
   One of the signs to pay special attention to is the inclination of all-out fatigue, which is then tracked by you falling into a profound sleep. This is not a similar quality rest that you ought to get for good wellbeing; instead, the aftereffect of these feelings is tired and exhausted.

2. **Negative Contemplations About Your Mental Health:**
   After this sort of assault, a few people begin having negative thoughts about themselves and examining their rational soundness. They consider that they are mentally weak and start thinking negatively about their normal mental health. This is another typical side effect of this kind of attack.

3. **Violent Bad Dreams:**
   Another sign that you have encountered an attack is the beginning of terrible or brutal bad dreams, especially if these are the kinds of thoughts you do not ordinarily have. This could incorporate side effects, for example, rest loss of motion and thinking that it is hard to breathe as a component of your dream.

4. **Unrealistic Dread Or Fear:**
   Some individuals experience a sentiment of extreme dread or fear for which there is no clear explanation and which might be going wrong. This dread can have a comparative impact of anxiety, making it hard to inhale and expand the pulse.

5. **Losing Control:**
   After this kind of assault, you may find that you lose control regarding your developments and thoughts. This is something that can cause you to feel vulnerable. Yet, you

can attempt to balance the impact through positive speculation to supplant the negative energy that originated from the assault.

Given our rushed ways of life, contrary energy, individuals, and feelings are very simple to stop by. In any case, by adapting yourself with a portion of the signs and indications of this sort of assault, you will be vastly improved to recognize and manage it.

Strategies To getting Rid Of Negative Energies
Negative energies influences ourselves and everybody around us. It restricts our capability to become a good human and something incredible and carries on with a satisfying, intentional life. Pessimism tangibly affects our wellbeing, as well. Research has shown that individuals who develop negative energy experience more pressure, more confusion, and less opportunity through the span of their lives than the individuals who decide to live positively and have positive thoughts.

When we settle on a choice to get effective and line that picks up with activity, we will start to experience circumstances and individuals that are likewise positive. The negative energy gets defeated by every single positive experience. It is a snowball impact.

Although negative and positive thoughts will consistently exist, the way to turning out is to confine the measure of pessimism that we experience by topping ourselves off with more significant inspiration.

Here are a few different ways to dispose of negativity and become positive.

1. Become Grateful For Everything

When there is something difficult to accept, consider we deserve what we have. A manner of qualification puts us at the focal point of the universe. It is a ridiculous desire that others ought to oblige us, our necessities, and our needs. This hollow reality to set yourself up is an unfulfilled existence of pessimism. Individuals living right now are "energy suckers"– they are continually looking for what they can escape. Individuals that do not value the distinctions of their lives live in a steady condition of lacking. Moreover, it is tough to carry on with a substantial life experience along these lines.

When we start to be thankful and value everything in our lives, we move our behavior from self-centeredness to appreciation. Others see this thankfulness, and a positive concordance starts to frame in our connections. We begin to get a more significant amount of that which we are aware of because we have delivered ourselves up to accepting, rather than taking. This will make your life all the more satisfying and progressively positive.

2. Smile More, Especially At Crucial Occasions

Life gets occupied; we get into task situated and schedule-driven connections. Being human can feel progressively like being a robot. This work-driven, genuine attitude frequently brings about negative thoughts and administration organized thinking.

It turns out to be specific methods of paying attention to life with positive effects and letting yourself free from all the pessimism. This is the leading life that you find a workable pace, not help up your mindset? Laughing encourages us to become positive by helping our state of mind and reminding us not to give it most of your time. Is it right to say that you are sensitive to light laugh? Do you experience difficulty laughing at jokes?

Typically, individuals who are worried and extremely genuine get generally irritated by jokes because their life is all about work, and their minds are not free of contrary thoughts. If we can figure out how to smile and laugh, life will be more significant in discovering what fulfills us. What is more, creating satisfaction implies finding motivation and positivity.

3. Help Other People
Pessimism is connected with narrow-mindedness. Individuals that live just for themselves have no higher reason in their lives. If the general purpose of this world is to deal with yourself and nobody else, the way to a long-distance satisfaction and intention will be a long one.

Energy goes with reason. The most fundamental approach to make positivity and inspiration in your life is to start getting things done for other people. Try to help others with their work or maybe with their problems. Start with the little work like opening the entryway for the others before you. Or ask somebody how their day was before telling them about yours.

Helping other people will give you an indistinct feeling of significant worth that will convert into positivity and inspiration. What is more, individuals may value you all the while.

4. Change Your Thinking Before Changing Others
Change begins from the inside. We can either be our best mentors or our best enemy. If you need to turn out to be positive, change the wording of your thoughts. A flood of negative self-talk is destructive to real and positive life.

Whenever you have negative energy, record it, and rephrase it with a positive turn. For instance, change an impression like, "I cannot trust I did so horrendously on the test." to "I did not work out quite as well as I wanted. However, I know I am responsible, and I will improve next time."

5. Surround Yourself With Positive People
We become like the individuals that we surround ourselves with. If our companion has negative energy and dramatization monarchs, we will copy that conduct and become like them. It is hard to be increasingly constructive when the individuals around us do not support or show actual conduct. As you become increasingly positive, your current companions will either welcome the positive version of you. Maybe they will get resistant to your positive changes. This is a characteristic reaction.

Change is terrifying; however, removing the negative individuals from your life is progress towards positivity. Positive individuals reflect their points of view onto each other.

Inspiration is a bit by bit process when you do it individually. However, a positive gathering of companions can be a help.

6. Get Into Action

Negative thoughts can be overpowering and testing to explore. Pessimism is generally joined by a "freak out" reaction, particularly when attached to relationships. Transform the negative worry into positive activity. Whenever you are in one of these circumstances, leave and enjoy a release. With your eyes shut, take a couple of full breaths. When you are quiet, approach the situation or issue with a pen and cushion of paper. Work out four or five activities or answers to start tackling the issue.

Removing yourself from negative by moving into the activity situated positive will help you tackle more issues judiciously and live in energy.

7. Feel Full Liability, Stop Being The Victim

You are liable for your thoughts. Individuals that reliably accept that things happen block themselves to a casualty mindset. This is a discreet and misleading negative energy design. Expressions like "I need to work" or "I cannot accept he did that to me" are markers of a casualty attitude. When it comes to taking full life responsibility, your thoughts & activities are perhaps the most significant in making an increasingly positive life. We have the boundless potential to transform us and change our thoughts. When we start to disguise this truth, we find that nobody can cause us to do anything. We pick our emotional and social reactions to individuals and conditions.

Famous Empaths

- ## Gem

The first empath on T.V. was Gem, who was featured in the first episode of the Star Trek series known as ' The Empath.' Here's her photograph. She was able to take upon herself the physical suffering of others. Finally, she died to save one of the company officials ' lives.

- ## Deanna Troi

Yet again, the following group of empaths in the media was on the Star Trek show. This time, it was the next-generation Star Trek. The first was a non-person, known as Deanna Troi, whose aim was to feel what other people felt.

- ## Tam Elbrun

The next passionate member of this group was Tam Elbrun, who appeared in the Star Trek The Next Generation episode entitled' Tinman.' He could not be around other people for long periods, and his life was too overburdening in nature. And he interacted with a living ship and finally stayed with it when he landed.

- ## Lwaxana Troi

Last but not least, in this Star Trek Trio was the mother of Deanna Trio, Lwaxana Troi, exhibiting the gift of empathy and telepathy, which is the ability through the connections of the mind, to interact with a person in both word and picture. She was a famous and continuous individual. After these Empaths, we hit another collection that captivated the audience for their wealth of detail. The ones I'm talking about came from the charming show, in which three sister witches had magic to help stop the dark.

• Prue

The first empath on Charmed was Prue when she spells a supposed innocent man in the episode named "The Primrose Empath," He fires back, granting him the power to feel the pain of the entire world at a time. The unintended gift so overwhelms you that you reverse fire and become very destructive. But in the end, she possesses the gift and can send it to the devil to kill him. During that episode, a new Empath, called Father Thomas, was imprisoned at one of the hospital's rehabilitation hospitals because nobody felt he had surrendered his humanity to a devil to save him from murdering innocent people.

• Pheobe

The next Empath was also from Charmed, but this hell, Pheobe, came naturally against Prue, who came on the empathy gift through a deceptive spell. This helped her understand what others felt and represented the talents of others as those talents were focused on empathy, something like empathetic reflection. She worked as a writer for aid and used her talents to support people worldwide.

• Peter Petrelli

We are now at one of the recent additions to this extraordinary Empath T.V. set. The gift of empathic imagery is said to be the ability to take on other skills and abilities by empathy for the Peter Petrelli of Heroes' show. Unlike Pheobe, which merely represents other people's experiences, Peter Petrelli absorbs and becomes his, too. This is something like a double of any power, while the original remains untouched.

• Jasper Hale

First, in a novel, by Stephenie Meyer, and afterward in the movie, Twilight. After all, it is the last Empath to hit the big screen as you can see from his picture; his name was Jasper Hale. Both the Witch and the Empath he's supposed to be. He can calm people's emotions when upset or depressed, but this only briefly relies on his closeness to the person he calms.

• Hilary Swank

In the 1999 film Boys Don't Cry, Hilary Swank is playing Brandon Teena. Hollywood actress Hilary Swank is coming at number five. In the 1999 film Boys Don't Cry, Brandon Teena, a transgender guy who has been raped and murdered by his friends after discovering that he has female genitalia, won her coveted place for her Oscarish role. Swank cut off her hair in the preparatory room and put on a cowboy's hat, wore her husband's clothing, and went to the streets of New York for a month to see if, like Brandon Teena, she could pass for a young man. She told her adventure: "Oh, what it is like for a transgender person, a lesbian or gay person! Swank's brilliant portrayal of Brandon Teena has contributed to raising the political profile of transgender peoples ' fighting and has also encouraged them to become campaigners in gay, lesbian, and transgender issues and spokespersons for the New York Harvey Milk School.

- **George Orwell**

In 1945 in Islington, north of London, George Orwell moved his adopted son, Richard. How can you get a Top Five Empathy without having George Orwell on the list? During his time as a colonial police officer in Burma, he gained empathy in the 1920s. Orwell was shocked by colonialism's violence he saw every day and learned what their life was like upon returning to Britain! He said,' I felt I had to escape from the reign of all humanity over other people, not just through imperialism.' He wanted to dress up as a tramp and live among beggars and vagabonds on the streets of East London, an era of his own life. Through this book, Orwell and its article on politics shone like no other writer in the twentieth century oppressed groups in British society.

Difference between Being an Empath and a Spiritual Healer

Empaths: are people who can perceive and truly sense other people's emotions. It is the ability to share emotions and feelings with others and to understand them. It is often known as being able to "put oneself in the shoes of another person" or experience the other person's feelings in some way. For example, if someone around you stresses you, you might begin to feel depressed even though there is an ambiguous reason to feel this way. This unique ability triggers parts of a neural network involved in processing the same state within you by a perception of another person's emotional condition, whether it disagrees, touch, anxiety, or even pain (think sympathetic pains or traumas). Empathy will search others' energy for emotions, experiences, and likely for events from past, current, and future lives. The characteristic of empathy is that they sense and tolerate others' physical signs because of their strong sensitivities. You view the world through your intuition and find it hard to intellectualize your feelings. Empathies are special individuals, extremely sensitive, and distinct from other men.

Empathies are the sensitive forms that change the interpersonal world; usually, friends and family cannot imagine being fun, caring, and understanding. Empathy is often drawn into work, which is very personal and makes a positive difference in other people's lives.

A **spiritual healer** is a person who becomes a gateway to healing energy and light. A healer has the power to "see" the entire person. The role of a healer is to help remove blocks for the growth of an individual. It is now widely recognized that all humans are electromagnetic beings and that the decrease in body frequencies below those required to maintain homeostasis leads to every disease. All fields are coherent by increasing the frequencies and the alignment of different bodies.

Energy therapy was long around and is one of the oldest treatment tools to keep the body safe and happy. The ancients were conscious that our thoughts, others, and unseen powers "out there" have had psychological and physical consequences. The alternative treatment of energy involved both physical as well as psychological dimensions.

These characteristics help you understand the direction with which you connect.

Empath traits
1. Feeling others emotions considering your own
2. Overwhelmed in public places, which can contribute to feeling or looking moody, nervous, aloof, or even disconnected
3. Watching certain violence, cruelty, or tragedy on the TV or in movies is unbearable
4. You know when someone is not honest
5. Digestive disorders, fibromyalgia, back problems, or prone to carry weight.
6. Always looking to champion the underdog

7. Excellent listener and others will want to offload their problems on you, even strangers
8. Under constant fatigue, with a need for solitude to recharge. A deep connection to nature
9. Prone to an addictive personality, Get easily bored or distracted easily if not stimulated
10. Creative, Drawn to healing, holistic therapies, and all things metaphysical
11. Love of nature and animals
12. Find it almost impossible to do something you don't enjoy
13. Strive for the truth, and always looking for the answers
14. Love of adventure, need for freedom and travel
15. Hates clutter on many levels (emotional, physical, energetic)
16. Loves to daydream, The ability to feel the days of the week
17. Finds routine, rules or control, holding
18. Intolerance to narcissism
19. Sensitive to the energy of food, antique items, and house dwellings.

Spiritual Healer Traits:

1. You are highly sensitive to energy.
2. You feel the emotions of other people as your own (empath).
3. You feel the ailments of people as your own.
4. You are intuitive & can read others very easily
5. A "big picture" thinker
6. Gone through the bouts of existential depression

7. You may feel like an outcast in your life
8. You think differently from others.
9. You get overwhelmed in public easily.
10. You are suffering from panic & anxiety attack
11. You are the natural peacemaker between people.
12. You are the confidant that others turn to when it comes to a needy period
13. You may experience digestive issues, gain weight around the stomach, or lower back pain
14. You may feel drain right after spending enough time with people around you
15. Sensitive beings just like animals & children gravitate towards you
16. Others tend to "dump" their emotional baggage onto you when it comes to dealing with
17. You may think in shades of grey
18. Aware of life interconnectedness & respect it
19. You believe in synchronicity more than coincidences.
20. You may have a history of healers in your family
21. You've experienced trauma in life, for example, loss of your family, near-death experience, and life-threatening illness
22. You've gone through a spiritual awakening.
23. May have experienced the soul of a dark night
24. You may have experienced chronic pain or an autoimmune disease
25. You are EMF sensitive (electromagnetic hypersensitivity).
26. Attract people who want to "fixing" but get trapped in roles like self-sacrificing
27. You're an excellent and compassionate listener.

28. Drawn to heal professions naturally that provide support to others experience balance & wholeness
29. You may feel distinguish between altering the energy within yourself
30. You have had numerous mystical experiences.

As you can see, with each characteristic, there are definite distinctions, but whether you are a spiritual leader or something else. You will need preparation so that these powerful gifts can be used, incorporated, and best articulated to optimize growth and profit via meditation, yoga, mindfulness, journaling, contact with nature, and motivation. Your only objective on earth is to love, which of course you do. You care for men, and you want to be happy, safe, and well embraced by all.

The overall experience of empath healing of a person

It is both a curse and a blessing to feel everything so deeply that feeling every bit of it. Empathy itself is not just living the experiences of various people. Still, it is defined as the act of feeling and understanding the energies people carry with them. These energies that some call vibes are a person's capacity to feel and reflect. Empathy is the inborn personality trait and lives within a person's instincts to observe other people's innermost thoughts and feeling as they feel. Empaths are silent observers of the world and what is in it, and they are not keen and sensitive about the humans only, but they are also close to mother-nature and its other creatures and creations.

Empath Healing Experience of a Person

Empathy can be a personality trait and a disease as well. Taking it into consideration leads a person to get sick in terms of being more emotionally sensitive and physically caring that he or she is lead towards hurting themselves. Empaths in their bodies are like those simple and caring people who do not think of their benefit and try to help everyone hurt themselves in the process. Calling empathy a disease is not suitable for some as it is not hazardous, empaths who are inwardly injured due to things they cannot stop doing, or due to things they are unable to understand. Sometimes in need of someone or something in this modern world to cope with their inner battles and struggles. Here is a detailed document on the empath healing experience of a person given below.

1. To heal from the inner injury of empathy, the first thing to do for an empath is understanding that one is not responsible for other people's physical downfall. Being an empath, one must know how it works with feeling everyone's pain and emotions. Sometimes, the person suffering from certain problems and pain does not work enough to get out of the situation, but the empath who suffers and tries his best to help the concerned person works more than the other. In this case, the empath needs to understand it entirely that they can do in boundaries. It is not their responsibility to make everything fall into place. It is not their mistake that someone is not getting out of an unwanted situation. It is often the case that the caring nature makes one blind because they cannot force a person to fix themselves if they do not want it or work for it. If they do not want to be fixed, one cannot bring them to the better side of life no matter what, and it is okay.

2. The second thing an empath needs to learn is getting away from the pain they feel is not to deal with it. One can never run away from a thing and cure it or deal with it. It seems counter-intuitive to get into the pain one is trying to get away from. Getting into the internal pain and emotional hurt that destroys inner peace and mental health needs to be understood first, and after that, it needs to be released. It is like a spring; if you keep pushing and do not leave a tip for sprinting it up, it will not let you be in peace.

When a person is preoccupied with running away from the pain, repressing the feeling, and avoiding the situation, they are giving leverage to this pain to get into the mind and senses more. The empath needs to sit down, relax, feel everything he or she is running away from. This is the foremost step to get away from the real problem and understand how to deal with all this confusion, hurt, and pain.

3. The next step towards healing an empath is significant for every empath who tries to heal from the pain they experience. Is it easy, straightforward to state that a person feels another's pain, which is the sole reason he or she is suffering from the internal battle? Is it of someone else, or is it their pain? Most of the time, the suffering individuals do not think of this before projecting the blame over feeling someone else that it can be them. A key feature is going through the healing process of empathy is detecting and distinguishing between their pain and the others'. It is the base consideration to heal from this pain and get a hold of it.

4. The next point to consider by an empath healing is the acknowledgment of the fact that low self-esteem does not work well with the healing process. One needs to boost their self-esteem to recover from the inner struggle and suffering they are going through. An empath with a high level of self-esteem makes it crystal clear how the healing process is boosted with this understanding level.

A person thinking himself to be worthless and unlovable is quite common, but empathy is confusing. When combining with the facts that one cannot help another person through tough times, these feelings of worthlessness and hopelessness increase this state of self-hate and underestimation. In other words, the pessimist thoughts of someone about themselves in empathy prove to be one of the significant reasons for suffering. The more love, respect, trust, hope, care, and affection one builds for himself make it better day by day to heal. Similarly, feelings of hatred make one think that empathy makes them so less valuable, which ends up hurting them so much in life that they become unstable in leading it and the empaths start saying, "They hate being an empath," etc. This situation can also take the person into another stream of thoughts confusing and hurting more.

5. There is a clear difference between having empathy & being an empath; it is loud and clear. Being empathic means feeling sorry for someone and being there for someone's needs. The difference is no one can see it, and it is just to be felt. They both make a person go through the same struggle and make him needed to be treated the same way.

6. Shielding is pretending to be immune to people's energies and their vibes reaching the empaths, but this is not the finishing point of the story as it is to be told that shielding is not an answer to the problem.

It may help the empathy for the time being to keep away from the energies, but it eventually leads to a high inner struggle and repressing the real emotions they feel, which further leads towards emotional injury. So the discussion concludes that shielding oneself from the energies of others does not work in the healing process of empathy. The empaths who are trying to get better need to face their emotional peaks without shielding and trying to cope with them, which is a long-term process, but it lasts longer compared to the shielding process. It is a time-consuming process to learn to avoid these energies that hurt an empath the right way, but it is also the most effective one. This is also called the non-attachment technique observed by the empaths in the process of healing.

7. There are some useful techniques referred to as the healing empaths in their journey to help them cope with their extra energies. The first technique is doing catharsis as much as possible at different times in a day. One can fix time for better treatment and consistency. Yes, the word habit is the best one for the catharsis point of an empath healing process because the recommended catharsis strategies are more like the good habits of daily life. These strategies include writing or journaling, going for a walk or jogging, exercising, yoga, meditation, laughing out loud, crying, screaming out loud in private, drawing or sketching, etc. To free the mind from extra heavy clouds of energy that the empaths keep, these are some of the best solutions for catharsis and removing extra stress.

The second important technique is body-mindfulness. This is what the modern terms call it, and its definition is in contact with one's body. In other words, it is taking care of bodily needs like nutrition and health.

8. The understanding of the fact that anyone can be an empath is less. The empaths themselves have this kind of understanding that empathy is for some specific people, and not just anyone can have it. The reality check is that empathy is normal, it is a gift that can be given to anyone, and almost everyone can feel as much in different fields and on different points. Domestication, social realities, norms, values, modernity, and other factors are the reason that does not let it bloom in every person. The empaths need to understand that they are normal, and empathy is natural, naturally healed. With this understanding, the empaths' journey towards healing will be clearer and easy

FAQs

Question: How can one tell a person is an empath?
Answer: The highly sensitive people and empaths have a lot in common, but there are a few differences between these two types of people. Empaths can absorb the energies of everyone around them no matter where they are from or what they do, and they feel as if they are standing in the shoes of the concerned person. On the other hand, highly sensitive people are sensitive about what they see someone going through or what they hear.

Question: How do I detect that I am an empath?
Answer: The most straightforward way of knowing if one is an empath or not is by reading different accurate things about empathy and relating oneself to it. If it does not work, various sites provide tests for analyzing if a person is an empath or not.

Question: Are empaths good or bad in relationships?
Answer: One of the major traits of an empath is being sensitive and caring, which gives the relationships a plus point that empaths can be the most loving, caring, affectionate, understanding, and polite in relationships though relationships for empaths are not an easy task, they can be highly effective if they prove to be a burden for them.

Question: Do empath suffer from depression and anxiety more than normal people?

Answer: yes, it is observed that the empaths are more likely to go through depression and anxiety episodes. Research says that people who suffer from social anxiety are more empathetic than others; it concludes that socially anxious individuals have more socio-analytic abilities than the people around them they get overwhelmed with this information and end up having an anxiety episode.

Question: Is being an empath just a story made up in my mind?

Answer: A book about empathy proves that being an empath is not just in people's heads. Instead, it is a physical nervous reaction, which is observed in ten to twenty percent of the whole population.

Question: Can I ever cure myself of being an empath?

Answer: Empathy is not a virus that can be gone by an antibiotic; it is said that a human being can be evolved into more sensitivity than less. So no one can get completely out of being an empath, but they can be healed with the help of some given strategies.

CONCLUSION

Empathy is not a disease; it is rather a way of life, a natural ability, and a way of feeling the world in a way not everyone does. It is the process of enduring all the energies of the natural being around. The empath ends up hurting themself, which is needed to be healed because it cannot be cured completely. This empath healing book gives vivid information on how to deal with empathy the best, which in short consists of the points of disconnecting from the hurting vibes, accepting themselves as they are, building up self-love, and higher self-esteem. Owning what is there in the person and loving it, not being responsible for other people's hurt, not shielding away the people's energies instead of feeling them and dealing with them. Distinguishing between others' emotions and their own and understanding that they are not outcasts instead of natural beings can deal with anything being normal because empathy is not something negative; instead, it is a blessing in disguise.

Printed in Great Britain
by Amazon